Two Contemplation Two Conten

The State of Northern Ireland and the Democratic Deficit:

Between Sectarianism and Neo-Liberalism

Paul Stewart, Tommy McKearney,
Gearóid Ó Machail, Patricia Campbell
and Brian Garvey

Vagabond Voices
Glasgow

© Paul Stewart, Tommy McKearney, Gearóid Ó Machail, Patricia Campbell and Brian Garvey 2018

First published on 12 October 2018 by
Vagabond Voices Publishing Ltd.,
Glasgow,
Scotland.

ISBN 978-1-908251-96-1

The authors' right to be identified as authors of this book under the Copyright, Designs and Patents Act 1988 has been asserted.

Printed and bound in Poland

Cover design by Mark Mechan

Typeset by Park Productions

The publisher acknowledges subsidy towards this publication from the University of Strathclyde.

For further information on Vagabond Voices, see the website, www.vagabondvoices.co.uk

Table of Contents

The State of Northern Ireland
and the Democratic Deficit:

Between Sectarianism and Neo-Liberalism

Prologue

With the range of profound social and economic problems facing our communities as a result of the UK opting for an austerity agenda to deal with the global financial crisis since 2007, this book will seek to address the current ways in which in Northern Ireland we are being hampered in dealing with the problems of UK-government-imposed austerity. The book is also concerned with exploring another critical structural feature of state and society impeding a broad, democratic response to neo-liberal economic policies: the new sectarian state of Northern Ireland.

One of the ways in which we are restricted is that the politics of neo-liberal economic policy have preferred a banker-friendly agenda of austerity which has deepened social and economic attacks on the welfare state. This we know, from whatever geographical point on these islands we care to stand. Furthermore, occasional rhetoric aside, this is also the accepted agenda amongst the governing parties at Stormont.

The other significant way in which we are hampered in our fight is a direct result of the ways in which the society in the north of Ireland/Northern Ireland has remained divided since the Good Friday Agreement (GFA) of 1998. Specifically, the array of social and economic concerns in our communities, deriving from a combination of neo-liberalism and neo-sectarianism, in our view have resulted in a profound "democratic deficit". Moreover, this notion goes beyond a recent and intriguing view that a "double transition" (to peace and neo-liberalism) has been under way since 1998. While the idea of a double transition takes us in the right direction, it remains limited by an economistic assumption that neo-liberalism is a problem that can be explained and challenged outside the problems posed by the reconstitution of sectarianism in Northern Ireland.

The reconstitution of sectarianism has taken place out of the smouldering embers of the old Orange state. One of our arguments is that what has replaced the Orange state is a new sectarian state that depends upon neo-liberalism: the old "economic sectarians" (in the shipbuilding and engineering sectors and the sidelining of working-class Catholic communities – together with a smaller Catholic middle class in the professions and small business community) have evolved into the new sectarianisms. The new sectarianisms in turn have been sustained under the watchful eye of a neo-sectarian establishment constituted by, and continually bolstered through, the strategies and actions of a new political class. The new political class comprises those who agreed that both sides had "won the war". The activities of this cross-sectarian dominant political class and economic elite operate in a way that sees it safely ensconced within its respective communities.

We can see the result of this process most prominently at the political level in the shape of a convergence between the political elites in the Unionist-Loyalist and Nationalist-Republican establishments; but the extent to which this convergence is economically sustained from time to time emerges into public view in the shape of political scandals emanating from Stormont. There remain significant differences between the two sides of the new establishment on a wide range of cultural and sociopolitical matters – although some might say their differences are not as profound as to present impediments to mutual backscratching – but on the crucial matter of the economy they both bend their knee to the same master. The master is, of course, neo-liberal economics and in our context its immediate manifestation comes in the shape of the UK state: however local spin presents it, the politics of austerity are driven by the neo-liberal government at Westminster. In describing the contours of the new sectarian state and society this book considers the playing out of recent significant aspects of the behaviour of the political-economic elite; the neo-liberal character of the economy in Northern Ireland and its impact both on long-term residents and those new residents, migrants mostly but not only from other EU countries, who came here after 2004; the constricting nature of sectarianism with society, Catholic/Nationalist-Protestant/Unionist-Loyalist; and the agenda for neo-liberal renewal using the third sector, supposedly to be developed following the nostrums of the Tories' "Big Society", and the way in which both neo-liberalism and the new sectarian society have eroded the space in which it was originally, and in many spaces remains, a vital bridge for social and individual survival.

These are all vital examples in helping us to deepen our understanding of the form and character of the new sectarian state in Northern Ireland; perhaps the profound nature of the democratic deficit is to be witnessed when we shine a light on those especially affected. As a means of furthering this objective we will try to shine this light on some of those affected by the conflict who tend to be ignored by the mainstream media. Finally, while we would assume that the immediate answer to the question of how to resolve the democratic deficit might be found in the labour movement, we will explore the extent to which it too is part of the problem. Telling us, as the official labour movement often does, that rocking the boat here – i.e. challenging the government over economic policy – will upset the peace process is cannily honest. Possibly uniquely so. It might just be that not rocking the peace-process boat is another way of justifying doing little to challenge one of the mainstays of neo-liberalism in Northern Ireland: the new sectarian divisions within the state and society. This is why we will argue that "peace" and neo-liberalism are not straightforwardly a transition from war but on the contrary have been quite easily reconciled under the umbrella of a new sectarianism. Neo-sectarianism and neo-liberalism are getting along together just fine. The democratic deficit has had, and continues to have, profound consequences for people across the north, whether in or out of work, whether living in a Protestant or Catholic community, or a community perceived to have no confessional affiliation of any kind. We will attempt to offer an account of some of the ways in which the democratic deficit can be challenged.

Introduction

A number of commentators have argued that despite the problems currently facing people in the north of Ireland, at least shootings are limited to the activities of an increasingly small minority of throwback loyalists, "bitter-end sectarians" according to Brian Kelly (2012, 4) and some republicans committed still to a military solution. A comforting thought, unless you are being shot at, based on the understandable assumption that just as civil conflicts begin earlier than is recognised they also blunder on much after their sell-by date, typically ending in a whimper if that is not how they began. It's not good but it will burn itself out, and any flare-ups are really just that – the last knockings. While the latest impasse witnessed by the threatened abrogation of the assembly – how many times have we been here? – represents the coalescence of a number of unresolved differences and contradictions, the script usually ends well. Old soldiers, of recent wars and none, after much hyperbole involving last straws, are metaphorically dragged shouting and belching to the Stormont tearooms once again. Even if this were to act as a source of solace it surely cannot suffice any longer when we consider that at the very least the constant threat, and on occasion the actual suspension of the "institutions", illustrate the sclerotic nature of the north, whether we are speaking of its ineffectual political class or its moribund political economy.

The central argument of this book is that the current problems in the north of Ireland/Northern Ireland can be explained as resulting from two distinct though related phenomena: a democratic deficit and a neo-liberal economic ideology. Both highlight significant failures of the 1998 GFA (aka the Belfast Agreement) which in its own terms remains incomplete. In the opinion of the authors, it could not have been otherwise, given that the dispensation it delivered depended upon a recombinant sectarianism, albeit one distinct from the former sectarianism that defined the Orange state.

We locate the origins of the present social and political malaise in two moments: the institutionalisation of existing patterns of sectarianism, now under the management of the Northern Ireland Assembly, and the emergence of neo-liberalism, re-energised after the crisis that began in 2007. There is a mutual dependence of one on the other. The new sectarianism, evident in myriad spaces and territories, from community activities and places where people live to particular small and micro enterprises, depends upon a careful management by the state and an increasingly diminishing public sector. While given significant support by Stormont, neo-liberalism, in other words, has been able to accommodate certain aspects of an earlier form of political economy dependent upon the older, better known, sectarianism. As will be shown, the capacity for neo-liberalism (with its customary mantra of regulatory anti-rigidity and economic flexibility) and sectarianism (rigidity and inflexibility per se) to mutually benefit one another is not a paradox at all.

Through the notion of the democratic deficit we will argue that the social and political resources essential in the north to confront neo-liberalism will only be visible when the central determining features of the new sectarian state and society are understood. From this perspective we are less convinced by the idea of the "double transition" to peace and neo-liberalism. This is because, as we argue below, the character of the ascendance of neo-liberalism in the north cannot in any straightforward manner be associated with the long-sought-for peace. On the contrary, embedded neo-liberalism has its own distinctive hue and moreover, far from thriving on the backs of waning sectarianism and political conflict, it is dependent on them in the north. Accordingly, we would question the idea, not only of the double transition but also the belief, prominent in some quarters – from the DUP (Democratic Unionist Party), UK Tories and, until recently, UK Labour – that peace will eventually arrive with greater economic performance under the auspices of more, not less, neo-liberalism (and it has been the preferred default for Sinn Féin and the Social Democratic and Labour Party (SDLP), champions of Private Finance Initiative (PFI). More than this, we also reject the notion that more peace will arrive with *less* neo-liberalism.

From our perspective, it is neo-liberalism itself which is exacerbating already parlous economic performance and deepening existent social and political conflicts. Furthermore, our argument begins from the view that neo-liberalism is not "out there", somehow rooted in transnational economic activities and still less those of finance, insurance and real estate (FIRE). These sectors and their various players are of course the drivers and the beneficiaries of neo-liberalism, but more than this, in the present context, they are being prosecuted precisely by the former sectarians who have morphed into the new supporters of the inter alia, international creditors, the shark-beneficiaries of PFI and the construction sector. The former champions of the older bigotries are in fact also our neo-liberals. This has been argued in Brian Kelly's article titled "Neoliberal Belfast: Disaster Ahead?" (2012), which makes sense of the relatively peaceful (maybe "relaxed" would be a preferable word) shift from old-style sectarian alliances to modern purveyors of the new economics. We would wish to go somewhat further, however. In highlighting the support given by the power-sharing executive to neo-liberal fiscal measures (for example, reducing corporation tax, choosing

PFIs and limiting poverty-reduction measures) both Sinn Féin and the DUP reveal something more significant about the evolution of the new state since 1998 and also something which has been less remarked upon until recently. Specifically, just as the older sectarians within and beyond the power-sharing executive have become central to the practice and discourse of neo-liberalism, to the same degree have they been central to the re-patterning and thus redefinition of what we mean when we argue that the peace process has delivered a new sectarian state.

Thus, it is not only that sectarianism and neo-liberalism may coexist but, more significantly, neo-sectarianism takes its revised form in neo-liberalism today. The buyers and sellers of the new economic orthodoxy from within existing communities look after their own in neo-liberal Northern Ireland in the way in which they did in the past. If the sectarian Protestant state gave us Unionist domination including better jobs and the like for one part of the community, while the Catholics took what they could of what remained (without denying the development of a small Catholic middle class), neo-liberalism offers a contemporary take on this older paradigm of sectarian community divisions. Finally, it is not only, as Kelly points out, that the "persistence [of sectarianism] is fuelled by continued and intensifying divisions on both sides of the divide" (ibid., 14). Neo-liberalism has redefined community divisions and played an important part in the evolution of neo-sectarianism.

This may appear odd since, as many enthusiasts have argued, neo-liberalism is to be understood as sweeping away the vestiges of tradition, which includes supposedly outmoded sociocultural and political forms. Yet, neo-liberalism is not an abstraction, and in concrete terms its impact on individuals and communities, keenly felt, can be easily measured as it confronts, negotiates and accommodates tradition. In the north, the promotion of free markets requires that notionally free labour is not so economically free that it can assert itself in the effort-reward bargain: wages must be kept low, and this is more easily achieved where workers cannot organise collectively. Collective organisation might appear so straightforward, a simple thing, so hard to achieve, and harder still where communities and sometimes families remain socially and culturally divided. Profound civil conflicts can present significant difficulties for capital of course, and for sure the long period of conflict in Northern Ireland hindered political and economic responses to the broader conflicts and eventual crises within the Fordism characteristic of post-war Keynesian states across Europe and North America that began in the early 1970s. Neo-liberalism was not about to sweep away the historically driven sociocultural conflicts of the north in any straightforward way since, in a number of instances, it made the problem worse. This is because the society which neo-liberalism encountered in the north was, all things considered, no less peculiar than any other, and in this regard, as happens everywhere, it embraced some social relationships and discarded others, while in some instances arguably worsening certain aspects of sectarianism. So, how to explain the current situation of impasse since 1989?

Before addressing the notion of the "double transition" (to peace and neo-liberalism) in Chapter 1, it's useful to highlight the kernel of the argument in the closing chapter to *The Provisional IRA: From Insurrection to Parliament* (2011), in which Tommy McKearney contends that while the struggle to break Stormont was successful in a number of vital respects, nevertheless the demise of the Orange state has given way to a new sectarian order:

> The nature of the capitalist state in Northern Ireland [...]
> in its Orange period, [...] was forged upon an indissoluble
> set of social, economic and political relationships between
> a dominant Protestant civil society and the latter's openly

celebrated repressive apparatuses. Together, this peculiar state-society configuration ranged from an exclusive Protestant housing policy, a gerrymandered political society, and economic, including employment discrimination against a Catholic minority. While the early movement for civil rights could engender a degree of cross-sectarian support, the nature of the Orange state and Northern Irish society effectively excluded the scope for the further development of a secularised opposition with the potential to affirm a progressive liberal, let alone a democratic socialist, agenda for change. (201)

We recognise that many on the left, including other socialist Republicans, have not simply been ambivalent about the outcome of the armed struggle, but positively unreceptive to any notion that it achieved much of significant value. Certainly, given the pitiful economic and political events of the last few years, wrought deep in the character of the GFA, it is hard to feel optimistic about the possibility of ever establishing a so-called "normal" liberal democratic polity. Even a minimum of what so many desire would at least be better than the present moribund state of affairs.

We respect the less than sanguine views about the legacy of the armed struggle and its outcomes including the GFA. We can see that however one interprets the circumstances, in truth the potential for progressive social and economic advancement often seems quite bleak, such that a political rejection of the long struggle that took place after 1968 has much going for it. Yet, while many of those we respect and work with hold understandably jaundiced views – and not only of the period of the insurgency and what it purportedly achieved – we nevertheless maintain that at minimum the insurgency effectively shone a light that eventually led to the collapse of the Orange state and its reactionary social, economic and political life. Though it seems a long way from 1998, even longer from 1968, a number of recent developments highlighting the importance of struggles and political agendas beyond sectarianism, rooted in community and labour movement politics, have begun to emerge. As we write, an early example of the way in which space has begun to emerge for progressive politics can be witnessed in the election of two formidable left candidates to seats in the Stormont Assembly, more of which later.

Yet, this optimism aside, we accept the daunting tasks that lie ahead for progressive socialist Republicans. It is hard to gainsay Bernadette McAliskey's argument, made during an interview with the *Derry Journal* in May 2016. She argued that while at least the "war" is over and that the mind-set based upon a never-ending cycle of war-and-betrayal in Ireland is receding (though still the only game in town for many), if only in the early stages of formation, the GFA allowed for new ways of thinking. For Bernadette, it was difficult to imagine what else the GFA had changed. In other words, what can we say has evolved significantly since the days of the Orange state?

> The only thing we really got out of the peace process in real sustainable terms was the absence of a context of political violence being the starting point of everybody's life. That was in many ways the same, just as a return to the equilibrium. And then people bring up the idea of power-sharing – but what power and what sharing? This is because the people who have not had the share of anything have been the most disadvantaged. They have nothing.
>
> At a very practical level the peace process and power-sharing was in fact designed for those in the middle ground. Now, in order to make it work Sinn Féin and the DUP have moved into the middle ground. That is the only reason it works.
>
> If Sinn Féin and the DUP had the same politics they had when John Hume and others were negotiating the peace, this

thing wouldn't work at all. So in order to make it work they have taken that middle ground.

In a sense they've stolen clothes of the other two parties, except that the reality is a bit like when you take the dissension that is created when both the DUP and Sinn Féin are arguing over violence and who is to blame?

The difference between them is that Sinn Féin politics only emerged gradually, they, at a time, didn't have a political coherence, so they haven't stolen the clothes they eventually just put them on. (*Derry Journal*, 13 May 2016)

There is little to dispute in this assessment. It is salutary and damning but there is also, oddly, a faint glimmer of hope in so far as it suggests that new progressive political spaces may emerge. We are at the end of war, we do not want to go back there (most of us anyway). This is more vital than we might at first imagine for it reminds us that while the war is indeed over, and that the DUP and Sinn Féin have developed their new middle ground, the territories they have abandoned are the living spaces and the agendas of concern of the working and non-working class in the north, though we cannot see that these agendas ever held more than a note of rhetorical interest for the DUP. For Bernadette, the GFA is largely empty because it has had nothing to say because "the people who have not had the share of anything have been the most disadvantaged. They have nothing."

Still, the "absence of a context of political violence" is quite some beginning and, though frustrating, the reasons for slow – painfully slow – progress are also now evident in ways that were not in the early 2000s. One of the aims of this book is to address the nature of the structural obstacles to a broad progressive socialist politics in the north, how these emerged out of the GFA, and the slow burn of an alternative agenda for change which ironically could only have arisen from the nature of the 1998 sociopolitical settlement. We will do this as we focus upon two aspects of the northern state, so far insufficiently brought together in the wider literature.

The first aspect we will focus on is the political and economic character of the new sectarian state. By this we are referring to the political and economic nature of the dominant groups (the DUP and Sinn Féin) in Stormont in terms of their success and failure. What is more, and an implicitly related theme, is that of social and economic decline and relative failure. By failure we are referring to more than the obvious deepening of social and economic inequalities identified by many labour movement activists and researchers. Usually trumpeted by the mainstream media as a success, the fruits of neo-liberal restructuring, including income inequality, employment degradation and poverty, widening on all dimensions, are as bitter as they are intended. Those who are lucky to have standard full-time jobs experience wage freeze or actual wage cuts, and their jobs will not only be cheapened for also they will be working longer hours and be under increasing pressure in terms of intensity. The negative outcomes in respect of different forms of physical and mental stress are well documented in the sociological literature of workplace stress. In the latest *Workplace Employment Relations Study* (Van Wanrooy et al. 2013) the most usual perception of change reported by employees was that they were having to work more for less money. Furthermore, thirty-two per cent of employees identified pay freezes or pay cuts as another feature of working life. When it came to their views on the quality of working life, twenty-eight per cent said that they had experienced an increased workload (Van Wanrooy et al. 2013, 8).

Those who do not have full-time jobs, if they manage to obtain jobs at all, will find themselves in precarious employment subject to a range of labour contracts including, at best, temporary full-time work, or part-time work including various forms of zero-hours contracts.

The second aspect which we will address later in the introduction is the presence of inequalities and sectarian divisions in the state that are shored up by older sectarianisms, kept well out of view – in "aspic" as we argue.

In the context of the developing decline (we use the word advisedly) of the North's own neo-liberal economy, it is worth taking a brief look at the extent of the general degradation of aspects of employment in the UK. As a region of the UK (whatever one may feel politically or culturally about this, the UK government rules our economy) the North's economy offers one variant of this. What is worse, the variant it represents has been described by a local wag as a mere shadow of its former self: declining manufacturing replaced by even less rooted capital in the service economy, typically represented by the sector emblematic of the new economy, the transient call centre. (Profile of a typical call centre: lots of public funding and a good tax regime, and the company provides low-paid jobs in a local economy; tax regimes and "tax regime shopping"/company accounting procedures impose increased marginal costs; firm shuts down having taken public revenue; unemployment rises again. Surprise/what surprise?) The data on the characteristics of employment trends presents us with a depressing picture throughout the UK and, as we shall see when we look at the North's political economy, things here are even more depressing. In a report titled *Hidden Work, Hidden Lives* (2008), the TUC Commission on Vulnerable Employment explored the degree and range of exploitation in employment and concluded that approximately two million workers were subject to various forms of insecure labour contract. The commission on vulnerable work presented a grounded and critical understanding of the basis of such work. This is work that is inherently vulnerable and moreover derived from, and characterised by, power imbalances between workers and managers.

This was in 2008. The 2015 TUC report presents data demonstrating the extent to which things have deteriorated further: "[At] the bottom end of the labour market, the struggle for a decent day's work in return for decent pay and conditions has intensified" (TUC 2015, 3).

And overall, the TUC pointed out that,

> According to the ONS survey of businesses, in January–February 2014, around 13 per cent of all employers had some zero-hours contract workers, but their use was more common among larger employers. Forty-seven per cent of employers with at least 250 employees made some use of zero-hours contracts, compared to 12 per cent of those with fewer than 20 employees. (TUC 2015, 6)

Noteworthy too, in terms of the growing importance of the third sector in the north, are the CIPD findings the TUC cites for the UK as a whole. The CIPD's data reveals increased use of zero-hours contracts, at twenty-eight per cent in the public sector, to be greater than other sectors while for the third sector (not-for-profits) it stands at forty-two per cent. Intriguingly it is in the private sector that we find the lowest use of zero-hours contracts – nineteen per cent (cited in CIPD report ibid., 7).

Yet, isn't it better to have a job than no job at all? The TUC report states that for the millions of workers on precarious contracts,

> mistreatment is the norm and where there is limited prospect of escape. [Moreover] those at the greatest disadvantage in society – women and young workers – are most likely to find themselves in precarious work. Of particular concern has been the sharp increase in zero-hours contracts and the widespread use of agency workers in the aftermath of the recession. Too often workers on such contracts face working conditions better suited to the Victorian era than 21st century Britain. (Ibid.)

The report further argues that,

> There is a clear link between casual employment and low pay. Those employed in precarious jobs tend not only to experience heightened job insecurity but also a significant pay penalty. Most have seen no benefits from the recovery. Instead they often find it difficult to make ends meet, with some resorting to pay day loans or even food banks to cover basic household bills and feed their families.[1]

As if deteriorating working conditions weren't bad enough, for people depending upon insecure employment, if they have any work, living conditions in the North also show a downward trend. In an April 2016 *Belfast Telegraph* article titled "Record numbers relying on food banks across Northern Ireland", Allan Preston reported,

> More people than ever in Northern Ireland are being forced to turn to food banks to feed themselves, with low incomes and benefit delays blamed for the increase. New figures released today by the Trussell Trust, who organise food banks across the UK, show foodbank use in Northern Ireland has hit a record high, increasing by 48% this year. The revelation has been blasted as "scandalous" with union leaders criticising the Stormont Executive's "failure".

Added to the problems of low wages and poor and limited nutrition, homelessness is again presenting enormous difficulties for thousands of our people. In a *Belfast Telegraph* article titled "Executive 'must do more to tackle unacceptable rise in homelessness'", Cate McCurry points to the Northern Ireland Housing Executive's (NIHE) own

---

1   The TUC report also cites the Office for National Statistics' *Analysis of Employee Contracts that do not Guarantee a Minimum Number of Hours*, published 30 April 2014 and available at www.ons.gov.uk/ons/dcp171776_361578.pdf

figures on the extent of homelessness, highlighting that, "Around 4,100 currently do not have a permanent home – a jump of 12% in the past two years alone" (12 November 2016). She goes on to state that,

> Research shows that [… t]he number of homeless people hit a record high, with the Northern Ireland Housing Executive (NIHE) spending millions of pounds every year on emergency accommodation. Statistics from NIHE showed that more than £4.9m was spent on housing people who were considered homeless in 2015 – an increase of £1m in four years. By March last year, 11,202 people were listed as being homeless, the highest number since records began. Director of Shelter NI, Tony McQuillan, said the figures exposed the "invisible homeless" problem" [sic] here. (Ibid.)

Finally – finally? – according to the End Child Poverty Coalition (ECPC), twenty-four per cent of children in Northern Ireland are "living in poverty" (*Belfast Telegraph*, 8 November 2016). The ECPC highlighted the fact that this is a Northern Ireland-wide problem, with the North and West Belfast and Derry areas presenting the most challenging areas. As an ECPC spokesperson said, "In each and every constituency in Northern Ireland, there are children being denied the happy childhoods and the good start in life other children take for granted" (ibid.).

Never mind, success for sure has been found for those, the minority, described by some such as Danny Dorling (2014) as the "1%", though it is somewhat broader than this and more like the top ten per cent, for whom increasing income inequality may on occasion be greeted with a mixture of satisfaction and anxiety: satisfaction to the extent that neo-liberalism has bestowed on them even greater treasures, and anxiety bred from fear of the possible consequences if the great unwashed multitude should decide to do something about it. This is becoming increasingly common across Europe and further abroad; in Northern Ireland it is distinctive in so far as the strategy has been to disburse this neo-liberal form of economic inequality in an even-handed manner between both the prods and the taigs. The mechanism for achieving this has been both unique, in a GFA kind of way, but also tawdry, in a more commonly recognised way, that is not so different from the kind of cronyism found elsewhere. It may be becoming more transparent, but it is doubly toxic nonetheless, since while it stands over more commonly understood forms of neo-liberal inequalities, it has tied the state and economy in the North into the highways and byways of more old-fashioned forms of sectarianism with what its beneficiaries regard as their little successes.

We argue that these are a necessary other feature of the new sectarian state: neo-liberalism and the new sectarianism go hand in hand.

The second aspect of the state we will explore is the way in which these inequalities and sectarian divisions depend upon keeping the older sectarianism hidden from view, or at best safely on display "in aspic" in the various museums around the North. This is achieved to some degree by reinventing the actual world of the northern state and society, of making it into something that it is not – or at least, of using the various glossy media images the NI tourist board wants to project in order to obscure the reality of the persistence of sectarianism.

To begin to tell the recent story of pathways to the centre of the new sectarian state may in some respects appear to be quite banal. Banal, if by this we mean the not so unique fact of patronage and brokerage in the manner of all dominant political formations in today's neo-liberal world. It is distinct though in that the patronage and community preferment comprise and sustain a story of two sectarian communities. Many, including Brian Kelly and Conor McCabe, from different socialist traditions, have made us familiar with a great part of the political economy of the contemporary sectarian state in the North. The story includes accounts of the rise of the new economies based on boosterism (a form of marketing aimed at hyping private and public policies assuming long-term community beneficiaries by which is usually implied jobs – see Kelly and McCabe on the idea that call centre jobs equal sustainable well-paid long-term employment); the cheapening of labour and the impoverishment of Protestant, Catholic and other communities (Kelly); and the role played by financialisation in sustaining the flight from the productive economy to the immaterial economy (McCabe). We want to add to their intriguing work an untold part of the story. Our departure may complement others to the extent that far from seeing the economy as failing because it cannot leave the war behind, to move properly to the now not so new world of neo-liberal transformation, the new sectarian state which arose out of the GFA sustains division by dividing the state largess between the "Protestant" and "Catholic" communities.

The question is not why the state fails because it somehow cannot leave the divisions of the past behind, nor that it fails because it does not look after its own communities "properly". We pose the problem somewhat differently – "success" is a relative word. For us the state in the north "succeeded", it "worked", and it worked precisely because of its relative success in disbursing state funds to its own defined constituencies. It succeeded until now because it had been largely effective in marginalising dissent whether it be still-at-war republicans or still-at-war and very pissed off Unionists (aka Loyalists, an often lazy way to describe angry working-class Unionists, as we will argue). In addition, because of the continuing cross-class character of the dominant sectarian alliances, the state and the dominant political classes together have been able to develop a hegemony for marginalising dissent – from

21

whatever its point of departure. This is a form of domination that blocks the spaces for broad, non-sectarian, working-class communities of varying progressive interests.

Of course, one-dimensional "Protestant" and "Catholic" communities do not exist in any simple, straightforward way, but the rhetoric expounding their reality matters. It matters especially due to the fact that it denies class and class differences which cut across sectarian affiliation within communities. It falsely identifies certain cultural aspects of our lives as markers designating "the other". Arguably the clearest manifestation of this is with respect to the Irish language, as can be seen in the bravely determined work of Linda Ervine, a language rights activist and Protestant based in East Belfast. This important work has seen her challenge many misconceptions regarding the relationship between the Irish language and those from a Protestant heritage who have forgotten, or want to forget – or would rather not know – the fact that Irish is the language of Ireland, not a religion. Ervine's role is especially significant given that while one side of her family was entrenched in a sectarian political agenda, most recently the Ulster Volunteer Force (UVF), another part of her family tradition, on her father's side, had a deep commitment to secular labour movement politics. Her father, for example, was a member of the Communist Party. Since 2011 she has organised and obtained funding for the Turas Irish Language Programme, based in the Skainos Centre on Newtownards Road. As she put it in a 9 November 2015 article in the *Irish News*,

> The more information I uncover about the links between my own community and the Irish language the more ridiculous it seems that I could ever have believed that I was doing something wrong by learning Irish. [...] To those who fear that learning the language will somehow change people's political viewpoint I would state that it has given me a renewed pride

in my Presbyterian heritage and made me more aware of the links between Ulster and Scotland.

Thus, describing communities in the north as basically Protestant or Catholic reinforces their confessional nature while denying space for others, as we will demonstrate when discussing the experiences of new migrants to the north. It denies the character of class subordination often revealed in the recreation of the social and psychological outcomes of the war, and the poverty attending this subordination. The latter is rooted in the enduring association of sectarian division with neo-liberal economy policies.

Our argument then is that "success" has been achieved thus far because cultural and ethnic identity has been privileged – and for now triumphantly so – over (cross-sectarian) class identities, as we pointed out above with respect to language campaigns. This is a limited success because to achieve hegemony, to block alternative narratives of what the state in the north represents today, means ironically either denying the nature and extent of social and economic problems facing so many communities, or more usually, denying their origins. The latter is important because if the source of continuing poverty, and community, social and psychological problems are denied, or interpreted in ways that obscure their origins in the long forty-year conflict, then in no meaningful way can we say that the GFA, with all its attendant sparkling new institutions and goodly words, can have succeeded.

The GFA has failed in at least two ways. First, in dividing the state largesse between the two dominant sectarian alliances, neo-liberal economic policies have hastened the increasing shift of GDP to capital and the dominant social classes, whether Protestant or Catholic, while leaving Protestant and Catholic working-class communities behind. This redistribution is typical through the global economy and notably where labour and social movements are weak and otherwise unable to stymie regressive redistribution (Dorling 2014). Second, since it must be obvious that the north is not "normal" in any liberal democratic sense of the term, by insisting on the fiction that it is, those who continue to suffer from the consequences of the conflict face a double indignity: their mental and physical suffering requiring specific means of treatment is denied through displacement on to conventional remedies, and since the social and political origins of their difficulties are denied – because they are told "the war is over" – they represent an embarrassment to a society which is in many ways still at war. We should be cautious in arguing that there is still a war, for it is obvious that in the usual sense of the word the war is undeniably over. However, while the civil war has been put in aspic and the military war is over, class war (this time, from above) is very much alive.

Society in the north is still at war because it remains a perpetually structured sectarian society; denying the continuing profound nature of sectarian conflict is not only an insult to those still suffering from the physical and psychological trauma resulting from the conflict, but also, in diminishing their trauma, society maintains their humiliation. "Don't mention the war. That's long past so get over it because Northern Ireland is a normal society."

Humiliation of those who have suffered and continue to suffer from the sectarian conflict, old and new, is meted out, albeit in different ways, to those excluded by the neo-liberal economic strategies. In mapping the key contours of the new sectarian state we will be highlighting the fact that the enrichment of some goes hand in hand with the increasing impoverishment of society as a whole. Using original research from a study of people in a working-class community in Belfast suffering trauma due to the conflict, the failure of the state will be revealed. As pointed out, while we now have a sure-footed critical political economy of the north, we still require an account drawing this together with an analysis of the architecture of the state: how it works in relation to society more broadly. Accordingly, our narrative will explore the political economy of the north; the impact of the new sectarian state and its rootedness in the historic compromise between the DUP and Sinn Féin; the current nature of Republicanism and Loyalism; and the changing balance between the state and civil society in respect of what some see as the retreat of the state through privatisation (described by some as "commodification").

This is in part a story about the rise of the third sector and its mapping on to the terrain of the north's sectarian state-society relationship. The patina of everyday sectarianism can be seen in the way in which the state dispenses its largesse. We will refer to those new citizens entering as migrants, and in relating some of their experiences we hope to shine a light on some of the peculiar ways in which the north, while seen by many as indeed normal, is normal in a very peculiar fashion. No account of the new sectarian state would be complete without an assessment of the role of the trade union movement, and we shall argue that a better response to ongoing economic crisis than the one currently being offered by the Northern Ireland Clinical Trials Unit (NICTU) is essential.

Conclusion

Sometimes, in seeking to show how a social and political system – in this instance the northern state – works, shining a spotlight on its various failures allows us to catch a glimpse of its special character: how does it do it? How can it function despite its abundant failings? In blocking its failures from view we can see that success has hitherto derived from its management of the marginalised and those who disagree (sometimes the same people). By illustrating its failure to defend its citizens as promised, and especially those amongst its most vulnerable, we will be able to get a better understanding of the dysfunctional nature of the state and society. We could do this in myriad ways but we have decided to focus on those marginalised by the conflict and specifically those carrying the mark of the past – people seen as failing in some way because they supposedly cannot move on. Their suffering tells us much about the pathology of the failure of the Stormont state as well as something about what we need to do to make things better. This book aims to account for what we take to be the current impasse in the north, a situation revealing a deeply unjust democratic deficit, yet we suggest some modest remedies that offer significant transformations which are both plausible and achievable. In most normal societies these would be viewed as basically reformist, but in the north, history and contemporary realities taken to the fore, they may presuppose far-reaching and – we hesitate to use the word – revolutionary change.

We reiterate however that the struggle against the Orange state was important not only because it did more than simply show to the world the nature of Orange repression. At the very least, and this is important to remember, it successfully broke the foundations of Orange sectarianism – anti-Catholic discrimination in housing, welfare, the economy more broadly, and politics. If the struggle was transformative it was so to a limited extent. It was necessarily also an incomplete war in reach and outcome. While the Orange state was being taken apart a new sectarian state was being remade under the auspices of the GFA. One outcome was that the anticipated peace dividend, as the parties to the GFA described the bounty that would be coming everyone's way if they gave up their guns, was greatly compromised.

The argument was then made that the so-called peace dividend was now profoundly limited by the stillbirth of the GFA itself. As some of us have argued elsewhere,

The price paid for the Good Friday settlement was reinforcement of sectarian social, economic and political divisions in the north [...] the sectarian state, supported by an international largesse in many ways protected from the deeper ravages of neo-liberal economics, has allowed for the development, largely within the public sector, of a new catholic middle class. [The] practice [of sectarian head count] encourages a crass form of clientelism favouring those closest to the party and in the absence of an effective opposition – a system almost without scrutiny.[2]

To seek to remedy this structural failure to produce a democratic, non-sectarian civil society, as a minimum, it is necessary to see the following:

• Open, transparent, democratic governance free from corruption and deceit: introduce one of the key proposals – a consultative Civic Forum – that was supposed to shape the new polity in the prospectus for the Assembly.

• Strong and inclusive human rights legislation which protects all members of society and is not subject to derogation. This was promised in the GFA and has not been delivered. Trade union participation in the development of community associations, tenants groups and women's organisations.

• Protection and enhancement of workers' rights though a range of measures subject to criminal law where these are breached. Monitored by MLAs and trade unions. Union membership of all publicly funded organisations.

---

2   This is quoted from two of the authors' (McKearney's and Stewart's) correspondence for a book on the Provisionals, and is available by request.

- Adequately resourced health, education and social care, free at the point of delivery and determined on the basis of need.

- Accessible and affordable housing; utilities (heat, light, energy, water) and transport for all.

- Fair (by which we mean progressive) taxation, in which the tax burden falls upon those best able to pay: the rich. Working people should not be made to pay for the corruption of banks, speculators and the government.

- A guaranteed citizen's income for the elderly pegged at the ROI and not less than twenty per cent below the national median wage to promote incorporation and participation in society. The multiplier effect on local communities will be significant.

While this list can be considered far from complete, the point is to argue that the peculiarity of the north, its divisive institutionalised political, cultural and political sectarianism, cannot be reformed by leaving the institutions of state as they are. Now, we might agree that these demands are not far-reaching enough. As the work of a range of critical researchers and writers has demonstrated, the straightened times since the global financial crisis of 2008 have allowed capital to deepen its offensive against workers and their families everywhere in which they are poorly or not at all organised. Moreover, dealing with economic exclusion and repression requires a political agenda that reaches beyond the limited democratic control of capital by labour and other progressive social movements. These demands can only be a starting point in the north of Ireland for the reason that we live in a Partitionist state, albeit one constructed in different (if also containing a number of depressingly familiar) terms from its predecessor, the Orange state.

Taking account of time, politics and the needs of our communities in their many guises, here is what we are certain of, and what we will argue in our strategic prognosis at the end of this book:

- A Nationalist analysis of any form cannot account for the problems assailing communities in the north today: it is an incorrect analysis, and to the extent that it has any social support in various places and communities, there is little enthusiasm for a return to any form of "armed struggle". Moreover, it could by way of contrast be argued that a deeper social and class-based analysis has potentially greater purchase in the right circumstances as can be witnessed by the success of anti-austerity and anti-capitalist social movement campaigns in some instances leading to successful contestation in democratic assemblies (in West Belfast recently and then more widely in the south).

- A socialist republic is a fine idea, and here is what it might look like today: Unionism is dead – long live Unionism! The older, Protestant, Unionism, defining the political form and character of the Orange state, has been superseded with the advent of the GFA whereby Catholics are now also to be Unionists in Carson's great "House on the Hill". Whereas in the past they had to suffer the indignity involuntarily, now they can do so with pride and no little conviction. Hegemony indeed. To break this system we require also a new unionism – trade unionism.

Chapter 1 examines the nature of the new sectarian state in the north of Ireland, assessing the argument that since the GFA and the deepening of neo-liberal economic policies, we have witnessed the increasing marketisation linked to a diminution of the welfare state. The chapter considers the view that the end of the new dispensation in the north can best be described as a "double transition" – to peace and neo-liberalism. Our argument is that while this has enormous potential to make sense of recent changes, including convincing data on the character of the North's political economy, the experience of a sometimes fragile peace together with the rise of neo-liberalism have been comfortably accommodated by the new sectarian state. Indeed, neo-liberalism and sectarianism have proved to be accommodating bedfellows. Our term for describing the current situation is that the north is suffering from a democratic deficit. Thus, from the vantage point of the political class, inward investors, various political elites, beneficiaries including Westminster, the state has been successful. However, considering what was promised in the GFA – the end of sectarianism, better job and community prospects, better and more inclusive citizenship – the failures have been stacking up. Thus **Chapter 2** examines the nature of the Northern Ireland economy in the context of neo-liberalism. It offers a particular focus on the plight of migrant workers coming to live here since EU Accession in 2004, highlighting aspects of their experience of living in a sectarian society seeking employment, sometimes against the persistence of sectarian labour markets. **Chapter 3** looks at the fate of aspects of the Unionist political agenda in its various guises, concentrating on the periodic (re)discovery of progressive Unionism. It highlights the failure of the latter to offer Protestant working-class communities a radical perspective for change since Unionism returns, as a precondition for its invention of differences with northern Catholic communities, to sectarian ideas of democracy. **Chapter 4** explores a broader failure of state strategy, the venal state, the failed state, and the disappointment of traditional Irish nationalism to promote a broad-based and inclusive perspective. **Chapter 5** considers the nature of the third sector which, though offering much by way of alternative employment, has been, or risks being, hamstrung – squeezed by reduced state and other financial support on one side as neo-liberalism bites, and on the other, by sectarian brokerage and patronage limiting the scope for community and other funding as defined by community affiliation. Continuing with the theme of political failure, **Chapter 6** assesses the attitude of the state towards those seeking emotional and personal security in the aftermath of the conflict. It's a truism to say that the measure of a society's humanity can be found in its treatment of the most vulnerable. Added to the stories of degraded work and employment, homelessness, and poverty, including child poverty, this chapter provides a brief account of the work of one mental health worker, giving testament to the lie that Northern Ireland exemplifies a successful post-conflict society. Unless, that is, our watchwords are "Don't mention the war". In that case, we can view the emotional and mental turmoil experienced by so many as merely effects of unfortunate but failed individuals. This chapter shows that, on the contrary, the poor mental health experiences of numerous people can be directly attributed to the long – and in many cases ongoing – conflict. Their struggles for good mental health are indeed hampered by a state response which we can sum up as one of normalisation. Not surprising when one recalls how the British state sought to portray the long years of conflict through the lens of a normalisation agenda: taking the political causes out of individual trauma is but a continuation of the older state agenda whereby the political conflict here was treated as if it was a game of bad guys against a good state, a game of cops and robbers. Usually, and for good reason, the response of the left would be to seek urgent support from the organised (and less well-organised) labour movement. **Chapter 7** presents this time-honoured solution as part of the problem. Labour will indeed have to be part of our solution but not, unfortunately, as it is now constituted. In this chapter, we demonstrate why the labour movement has been hampering the kind of significant change required to transform the north into a progressive society. Breaking its obeisance to the new sectarian state would be a vitally important starting point.

Chapter 1

Sectarianism and Neo-Liberalism: The New Democratic Deficit

What is the best way to describe the north of Ireland/the six counties/Northern Ireland today? What kind of society cannot call itself by a commonly agreed name? A society that is not its own, perhaps? Perhaps in the end, agreeing on a name does not matter. Perhaps, perversely, the plurality of descriptors for the place is a healthy sign – it certainly gives us something to joke and laugh about. And anyway, we are not all shooting one another over it – or at least, not as much as we used to. Then again, perhaps it does matter, but in a way that is not so funny: maybe not being able to agree on what we call our homeland is an allegory for other troubling divisions. It could be argued that this lack of commonality reflects other weakened, possibly non-existent, social solidarities, and that this very absence makes possible the kind of sclerotic political culture that others profit from. Let us make clear at the start exactly who and what we are referring to when we talk of others profiteering from an absence of political control of our place: we are referring to those who run multinational companies, government agencies in Westminster and Stormont, and our local political class.

To add to this beginning of an answer we could do worse than trying to make sense of where we are, of what has happened to the north since 1998. An important recent explanation for the various processes of change – one that gives some grounds for optimism towards progressive social and political forces – is provided by Conor McCabe in his intriguing concept of the "double transition" (2013). By

33

"double transition" is meant the transition "towards peace and neo-liberalism" (1). McCabe's view is that neo-liberalism (in terms of privileging finance, insurance and real estate)

> is being treated in Northern Ireland today as if it is somehow part of the peace-building process. The assault on public housing, the campaign for devolved powers on corporation tax, the privatisation of public services: in all of this we are witnessing businesses that are parasitic in nature – i.e. finance, insurance and real estate – being given privileged status and political backing by the power-sharing executive. (16)

Moreover,

> This double transition – towards peace and neo-liberalism – has been mediated through the world of politics, finance, law and accountancy. It is the financialisation of the economy that demands low pay and privatised services, not geography, history or conflict. The rent-seeking profit model of financialisation has been put forward as a solution – in fact it is often hailed as the only solution – to the deep social and cultural conflicts at the heart of Northern Irish society. In fact, financialisation is antagonistic to the type of social and communal relationships necessary to develop and sustain Northern Ireland today. Nowhere is this seen more clearly than in the policy of public-private initiatives and partnerships, or PPPs. (4)

Thus we can see the attraction of the idea of a double transition in so far as it neatly captures a number of aspects of the state of the North since the outworking of the 1998 GFA. While signalling incompleteness in the evolution of state and society towards peace since the end of the nineties it also reminds us that there remains a lot to do before the "peace" returns fully. The argument that the movement from war to peace is now being accompanied by the movement towards neo-liberalism is a powerful one and an important corrective to the great wish fulfilment carefully cultivated by various media outlets declaring that the war is over and we need to get on and make money – claiming "peace brings with it prosperity", as if all benefit to the same degree, forgetting some are not benefiting at all. As well as neatly flagging up what remains to be done, double transition also suggests that many people, not least those who have suffered most, are being materially short-changed, losing the most as well as being excluded in myriad other ways. Double transition, in other words, highlights the extent to which the peace itself, however one understands it (though for us it is an imperfect peace), is being accompanied by a significant widening of class inequalities, deepened by state-driven neo-liberal economic strategies.

Nevertheless, and with respect to the thoroughness of the political economic critique suggested in double transition, our difficulty with it, finally, is that it reduces social, cultural and economic phenomena to secondary importance in critical political economy analysis. It is true that double transition recognises social and economic issues. However, it does so in a way we feel is subordinated to its focus of analysis. One problem with the concept is that while it highlights the contradiction between neo-liberal policies driven by the needs of FIRE and community cohesion – FIRE destroys communities, basically – it underestimates the extent to which existing patterns of political and economic subordination coexist with (and in critical instances depend upon) the perpetuation of neo-sectarianism. While it is often true that we can say, "It's the economy, stupid," it's also true that the social and historical context – the history of local political economies – drives the embedded nature of economic forms of social and political organisation and relationships.

Unless we take this on board, we might think that while "it's the economy, stupid", this should be taken literally to mean that economic, as understood in orthodox explanations, is all and that whatever gets in the way of rational economic moneymaking is not only a drag on neo-liberalism's rationality but, for that very reason, is doomed to disappear. The analysis here suggests that neo-liberalism has to be understood as being embedded in the societies and economies in which it is being pushed forward. That is to say that since neo-liberalism is not an abstraction, the economic patterns, the social and specific patterns of exploitation established by it, will start from the society in which it finds itself.

Unless we begin from the given society in which neo-liberalism is being studied, we run the risk of saying that capitalism is everywhere and eventually the same. It is true that capitalist development can be understood as reducing tradition and opposition in the face of advancing modernity, but this is only part of the story. While neo-liberalism rests more easily on the fat legs of the neo-liberal bourgeoisie in South Africa, Brazil and the United States, to take just three examples, since the coming to power of the ANC, Brazilian social democratisation and the election of Obama, no one for one moment supposes the end of Apartheid has seen the end of social apartheid, that the rise of Partido dos Trabalhadores (PT) – Workers' Party has brought an end to social cleansing, or that racism is dead in the US. How many gunned-down mineworkers, how many shot-down social-movement leaders and poverty-stricken peasants from Brazil's far north, and how many shot-in-cold-blood young black people in the US do we need to witness before we know that all of these not only sit comfortably with neo-liberalism but indeed are sustained by it?

In the north of Ireland sectarianism not only rests comfortably with neo-liberalism – it is sustained by it. Our view is that the particular shape of the new sectarianism in the north is dependent upon a particular form of neo-liberalism. We leave open to discussion the extent to which sectarianism deepens the latter, but we do argue that the former, the new sectarianism institutionalised since 1998, is tied to a particular form of neo-liberalism. It is in this sense that we argue that rather than seeing neo-liberalism as simply one overarching economic form in some way understandable in an abstract, pure, sense, it can better be understood as a form of political economic orthodoxy taking variant forms in each state. We term these varieties of neo-liberalism. In the north, the economic orthodoxy that began to have an impact beginning in the 1970s, increasingly privileging the role of finance and the banking sector, was driven by housing and, of course therefore, the building sector – just as it was in the rest of the UK, the Republic of Ireland and a number of other countries, including the US and Spain. These were, now famously, the countries hit hardest by the spectacular financial crisis that began in 2007. But housing, housebuilding and construction were not at the root of the financialisation of the economy, though they were the particular form taken by financialisation in these countries.

While this all makes consummate sense, it also may be said to underestimate the persistence of sectarianism within the social structure that cannot be straightforwardly limited, let alone excised, by liberal democratic reforms. Of course such reforms are important, but their limitations are defined by context. In the perspective elaborated upon here, instead of joining in the popular argument that the north is transitioning to peace – a peace somewhat tarnished by the waste of neo-liberalism – we will show that the idea of transition itself is problematical. More specifically, we will argue that it is the persistence of sectarianism which is limiting peace, or rather, contriving a particular kind of peace – the war is in suspended animation – and finally that this sectarianism, far from being incompatible with neo-liberalism, is furnishing it with a new-found vigour. In short, sectarianism and neo-liberalism are making fine bedfellows. This is based on the argument that the new sectarian state is one of the outcomes of the GFA and that this goes beyond parliamentary protocol, reflecting as it does, deeper social structural imperatives beyond the comfortable confines of the Assembly.

The new sectarianism allows for weaker labour organisations, which otherwise may challenge capitalist restructuring. It weakens communities that might resist marketisation and commodification. In other words, weakened trade unions and riven communities find it difficult to resist – if they even imagine resisting – recommodification of the public and wider social realm whether it be hospitals, state employment and other services together with other aspects of the social wage. To see sectarianism (a form of racism) or other social divisions as being inimical to the varieties of neo-liberalism brings the risk of confusing its radical modernising agenda, its creative destructive character, at the heart of all forms of capitalist renewal, with a progressive social and cultural ambition. It is almost as if neo-liberalism is being counterpoised – and therefore with a small element of historical progressiveness? – to sectarianism. The iron wheel of late capitalist development will beat away the historically reactionary sectarianism in the north. If only it were so straightforward.

Neo-liberalism, like all forms of capitalist political economy, is contradictory in its socio-spatial origins, processes and trajectories, and while the making of value and profit from finance can find little local difficulties unhelpful in the pursuit of profit, these little local problems may also assist its objectives by dividing the peasants and setting them against each other. It all depends on local history, labour and community formation, bolstered as these are historically by state strategies, and social and class alliances. After all, was it not the case that the darkest period of sectarian conflict took place when the UK and the north were at their most deeply social democratic? The issue then is not so much the antipathy between neo-liberalism and other supposedly backward social and cultural forms, but rather how to understand the recombination of sectarianism and the new pattern of capitalism – neo-liberalism with its embeddedness in financialisation, state-sponsored privatisation, and institutionalised sectarian political and social divisions (Garvey and Stewart 2015).

Finally, one of the critical weaknesses of the GFA arises due to the neo-liberal restructuring of the sectarian welfare state economy of Northern Ireland (SWSNI). It is the nature of this SWSNI that matters and which makes problematical the prognosis of the double transition. In the first instance we describe the nature of the SWSNI before identifying the nature of the political economy of Northern Ireland and the rise of neo-liberal employment and work regimes as the North emerged from a protracted civil war stretching back more than thirty years. In terms of strategy for addressing a relative deepening of cultural, social and political sectarianism, we argue that it will be better to concentrate on the democratic deficit. This suggests that rather than a transition, considerable political gains are required, and that these will need to go beyond both the current political establishment and the political processes characterising the north: democratic deficits present themselves at the level of employment and the workplace, the community and wider social relationships that require transforming. First, however, let us recall some detail of how what now passes for normality came about.

The sectarian welfare state economy of Northern Ireland[3]

This is a story, in part, of the sectarian welfare state meeting the new era of neo-liberal transformation in which the old social settlements of 1945 (the rise of the Keynesian

---

3   Several passages in the following section were prepared for Garvey and Stewart (2015).

welfare state) and 1998 (GFA) have been disrupted, if not (yet) abandoned and face an assault from the new tide of neo-liberalism being dispensed by London and the Northern Ireland Assembly. This is because, in addition to communities facing the neo-liberal challenge, a new political class, with its roots within the communities, was given institutional backing in 1998 and together with the attendant social and economic relationships supported by the state, is under threat from UK neo-liberal state strategies. This is important to note because state and society in the north still reflect enduring social divisions founded on a historic compromise between the dominant parties of Ulster Unionism and Irish Nationalism which the new political class reflects.

The SWSNI has had two phases. SWSNI-1, beginning after 1945, was marked by the adaptation of British Keynesian welfare state strategies designed for social and economic inclusion to the institutions of the Northern Ireland Orange state, *sui generis* (O'Dowd, Rolston and Tomlinson 1980). Keynesian policies of social inclusion sat, antagonistically, alongside the state's repressive apparatuses founded upon the social and economic exclusion of northern Irish Catholics (inter alia, Coulter and Murray 2008, op. cit.). While the civil insurgency which began in 1968 would effectively end with the harnessing of this particular pattern of subordination, the UK government extended elements of Keynesianism in order to maintain employment in the face of social and economic sclerosis accompanying the civil insurgency. This was a key feature of the second phase, SWSNI-2, which began in 1998 with the GFA, and it has been marked by the institutionalisation of sectarian political structures that, far from depending upon Catholic exclusion and subordination, rely, ironically, upon the subordination-by-inclusion of both Protestant and Catholic communities, qua Unionist and Nationalist political identities. This is codified by the D'Hondt principles defining the distribution of political power and patronage in the Stormont Assembly. This has depended upon the creation of what has been described locally as an new political class (Shirlow and Murtagh 2006; Shirlow 2012) that provides the social and institutional relationships with significant leverage over the targeted disbursement of state (EU, UK and Republic of Ireland) funding for those community associations linked directly or indirectly to Protestant or Irish Nationalist community networks: in local parlance, "the price of peace".

Specifically, the European Union special PEACE Programme for Northern Ireland allocated €333 million in strategic PEACE Programmes between 1995 and 2013. During the 1995–1999 period some 13,000 projects received support and the special programme included a specific budget for ex-prisoner groups to encourage "conflict prevention and transformation". By 2003 a total of sixty-one political ex-prisoner groups and a further twenty-nine affiliated projects received €9.2 million from the EU PEACE funds (Shirlow et al. 2005), reflecting both the high percentage of the population who are politically motivated ex-prisoners (fourteen to thirty-one per cent of the male population according to Jamieson, Shirlow and Grounds 2010) and, by offering a stake in the new dispensation, sustained political concern for the survival of the "peace process" (McKeever and O'Rawe 2007).

Estimates of the number of people directly and indirectly involved in the conflict vary considerably. Yet, what kind of citizen is it possible to be in Northern Ireland if one cannot be defined as a Protestant or a Catholic – a problem confronting many workers arriving from outside the UK whose entry as new workers has turned a light on both the fragility and the continuity of the social settlements. Many migrant workers' experiences of exclusion illustrate the extent to which a range of institutions, living spaces and communities in Northern Ireland reproduce the exclusionary sectarian practices developed during both eras (SWSNI-1 and SWSNI-2). This may be ignored in a number of technocratic labour- and union-focused policy responses since the hegemonic reformist trade union perspective has tended to isolate the citizen's "problems of the civil war" from the worker's "problems of the class war" (Shirlow and Murtagh, op. cit.; O'Dowd, Rolston and Tomlinson 1980). Historically, as is typical, focus was trained on the latter while the former could be hidden from view ("Don't talk about the war"), with implications for the "new" workers as documented here.

By 2008, 25,000 public sector jobs had been created since the GFA, and the region was enjoying the greatest increase in employment in the UK, with 10,000 new jobs per year being created (DEL NI 2009). Economic inactivity levels in certain working-class neighbourhoods, however, remained stubbornly high. The manufacturing and hospitality sectors were among the key destination workplaces for migrant workers, and these typically lay outside of organised union sectors and specifically the public sector, especially with the decline in traditional, male, blue-collar employment (shipbuilding, engineering and aircraft). Again, their concentration in low-skilled and low-wage jobs despite a relatively high level of education is consistent with findings across the UK (ONS and DETI 2009).

Many of the labour-process issues that workers confront currently result from the intensification of work, increasing casualisation and insecurity (and some hostility from locals) typical of this current phase of neo-liberalism. According to the May 2016 Northern Ireland Labour Force Survey (NILFS), with an unemployment rate of just under six per cent, 323,000 people are either unemployed or unavailable for work, but what stands out from the NILFS, and as great a concern, is the fact of long-term unemployment, where the NILFS data show that 60.8 per cent of people receiving unemployment benefits have been on the dole for more than twelve months – an increase over 2015. Moreover, the picture for those under twenty-four years of age was still grim, with 18.1 per cent of young people unemployed, the highest by far in the UK, where the average rate currently stands at 13.3 per cent. In a 12 November 2015 *Belfast Telegraph* article titled "Stagnant Northern Ireland economy raises fears for long-term unemployed", Danske Bank chief economist Angela McGowan is quoted as follows:

> The number of monthly claimants is continuing to fall, which is great, but if we scratch below the headline indicators it is clear that Northern Ireland is still struggling to create enough new jobs and has a very serious long-term unemployment problem.

The NILFS report goes on to highlight the additionally worrying percentages for those on the dole and benefits: those unemployed drawing the dole for more than twelve months (long-term unemployed) was 60.8 per cent (an increase of two per cent on the previous twelve months). Wonderful!

Worker insecurity, depending upon a range of exclusions, including unemployment and weakened welfare support, is never intelligible without proper recognition given to the attack on labour organisation. The broader political economy background here cannot be ignored. Financial and labour market deregulation typically depend upon the assault on labour standards and the fragmentation of labour markets (rise of temporary, fixed-term, sometimes zero-hours, contracts), which are made possible to a considerable degree by the weakening of labour unions. A significant feature of contemporary globalisation is governmental, company and wider ideological antipathy towards the barriers and protections to insecurity sought by trade unions. In other words, neo-liberal globalisation has at its centre the axis of labour market deregulation (inevitably allowing for other forms of social and economic control) aligned with the liberalisation of financial markets. (See Harvey 2010 and Standing 2009 for a more in-depth discussion of this.)

The North has until recently been the recipient of levels of public spending well in excess of the rest of the UK, reflected in a higher proportion of public sector employment (32.3 per cent) compared with the UK average (21.1 per cent). While a higher level of public spending than elsewhere was initially a response by the British state to the impact of the insurgency on capital formation and employment, the GFA laid the basis for sustaining higher levels of expenditure on both capital and the provision of some £500 million (Ruddock 2006) for the so-called peace dividend. This provided an important underpinning to the new post-conflict political class that was vital in maintaining the Keynesian welfare state in Northern Ireland (Coiste na n-Iarchimí 2003). Not only has the 2008 crisis been undermining the foundations of SWSNI-2, but the UK government's solution during David Cameron's Big Society venture imperilled the full range of local post-conflict resolution programmes accounting for the employment of 27,000 in SWSNI-2 (NICVA 2009). To add to this, since Theresa May's Tories have been in power, beginning in 2016, public sector provision and employment via privatisation and outsourcing continue to be attacked, and so are those state-funded community programmes defined largely by the post-conflict employment regime underpinning the new political class. The impact of Brexit will deepen the crisis experienced by a range of public and third sector organisations.

Chapter 2

The Global Economy and the North of Ireland: Neo-Liberalism at Home

The stark social inequalities that fuelled the "Troubles" remain deeply entrenched: the very same districts that suffered the brunt of the violence from 1969 onward remain at the bottom in poverty, unemployment, and social deprivation; public funding is being cut to the bone, with hospital patients dying on trolleys and schools facing closure [...] All this is being carried out by an Assembly at Stormont that seems to be constantly falling out over issues having to do culture and national identity, but is ecumenical enough in its collective worship of the free market.

– Brian Kelly (2012, 2)

The rise of neo-liberalism has to be understood as taking particular forms which derive from the history of social and economic development in each space and territory. In the north, neo-liberal economic policies depend upon the persistence of neo-sectarianism. Kelly makes the argument that jobless growth has been central to economic development in the north (we understand this to be characteristic of neo-liberalism more widely), and his additional and intriguing point is the notion that the north is being shaped as a special economic zone.

Despite some great propaganda by Sinn Féin, speaking at times to a left constituency, in practice the party is wedded (today) to the neo-liberal economic strategies outlined here. Wonderful wall propaganda is meaningless in the face of a set of policies-in-practice bowing to the might of the neo-liberalism described throughout this book. This is especially disappointing when we turn to the consequences of neo-liberalism on peoples' wages and conditions of employment, including the nature of the work people do (when they have jobs), their housing and their health, all of which impact profoundly on someone's ability to participate in a democratic society. More than this, the inextricable links therefore between weak public engagement and disempowering work and employment relationships sustain the deepening poverty for a significant number of people. So, the "success" of neo-liberalism for the winners is boosted by the weakness in civil society of public engagement, something that was supposed to change in 1998. It is in this sense that we discern the roots of the North's democratic deficit.

The reported figures describing the nature of increasing wage impoverishment in the North are compelling. John Mulgrew of the *Belfast Telegraph* reported what he described as a "double-digit dip" for average pay in the UK while here in the North there has been a five per cent wage decline in seven years (*Belfast Telegraph* 2015). Furthermore, according to Mulgrew, citing the economist John Simpson, wage decline was slightly lower here and wages had "flatlined" due to the fact that there are fewer high-wage earners in the North who have access to "overtime and bonuses".

If this tells us something of the situation as regards falling wage rates and living standards in the North, what of the overall picture with respect to the nature of work, employment and wages in comparison with the rest of the UK? Did the 2008 global crisis affect the north in ways distinctive from the rest of the UK, and what would be useful measures by which we might judge the differential impact of the crisis in the north? What is the reality of the North's neo-liberal economy? This means that we need to know what measures we can use to assess whether it has performed worse than the rest of the UK since the 2008 recession. Paul Mac Flynn's research into hours and earnings (2014) together with that by the Joseph Rowntree Foundation on poverty and social exclusion (Tinson and MacInnes 2016) get to the heart of the problem of the North's ailing economy. These figures describe a set of circumstances, a political economy that is inherently dysfunctional – for many people but certainly not for all. The poor work and employment that many people experience (see above – precarious and degraded work often attended by low pay) are not accidents that can be addressed by minor tinkering of the system.

Deregulation allows what many experience as dreadful working conditions and eroded employment options to prevail. It is supposed to be this way. It is good that as a result of research by the JRF, we know more now about these conditions and their consequences in terms of poverty – including poor housing, a degraded social fabric, hyper social and economic exploitation, and increasing racism – but let us not assume that employers engaging in such practices do not know about the importance of low pay and deregulated work and employment: they like it this way. What they do not have a great deal of concern with are the social and economic consequences of neo-liberal employment regimes.

In this chapter we begin by looking at the figures describing the extent of the neo-liberal economic depredation here. We then assess the effect of economic changes on jobs, including changes to the type of work people are increasingly engaged in. We also take stock of some Joseph Rowntree research into the extent and form of poverty, and finally, we consider some migrant experiences of life here.

The North's new-not-so-new economy

Let us take a look first at Paul Mac Flynn's findings in *Hours and Earnings in the Northern Ireland Labour Market* (2014). Mac Flynn explored the consequences of the 2008 recession on jobs and pay in the north. His results are striking. Based upon an assessment of working time and pay the picture he draws is one of a skewed economy overly reliant – in our view – upon precarious, low-paid employment. Comparing the North with the rest of the UK, he highlights a number of trends that characterise the nature of the precarity. Mac Flynn is concerned with exploring whether the rise in new types of jobs and weakening labour standards (i.e. a rise in "low-paid and precarious employment") "could disguise an underlying weakness in the Northern labour market" (3). He argues that while the North's economy has a closer resemblance to the Republic, for obvious reasons, there are significant variations from the UK. His analysis is revealing:

> Northern Ireland along with all other regions of the United Kingdom saw significant falls in employment from 2008 until late 2012. Since then employment *levels* have trended upward but employment *rates* have remained more static, particularly within some groups. [...] [W]hile overall numbers employed has recovered beyond its 2007 level, correcting for population increases the overall employment rate remains the same. This means that while Northern Ireland may have the same number of people in employment as it did in 2007, that cohort is a far smaller section of the total population and as further breakdowns show, it is a very different cohort to that of 2007. (4, emphasis added)

The following findings are also illuminating:

> Employment levels for both men and women have increased following a substantial decrease in 2008, and employment levels for men have now almost reached their 2007 number, while employment levels for women are significantly above 2007 numbers. However looking at employment rates paints a much different picture. Male employment rates have fallen by nearly 5% from 2007-2009. As of 2013 the rate is still

3% below 2007 level, indicating a significantly reduced male share of total employment. In contrast the female employment rate, despite a drop in 2008 is now almost 2% higher than it was in 2007. This is the first significant shift in employment, from male to female. Importantly though [...] female employment is far more susceptible to low pay and uncertain hours, and thus has implications for the labour market as a whole. (4-5)

His data on work and employment echoes that of the TUC (2015) above, as well as that of the Joseph Rowntree Foundation (2016). Comparing the rise in part-time work in the North with the UK as a whole using Labour Force Survey Northern Ireland & Labour Force Survey UK 2007-2014, he argues,

the rate of part-time employment and consequently the reduction in full-time employment in Northern Ireland has been in the order just under 4%. In contrast the change in the part-time full-time ratio among employees in the UK as a whole has been over 1%. (7)

And, of course, indelibly tied to poor jobs and poor employment is low pay: these are key causes of "poverty and deprivation" (27). What is more,

Northern Ireland is the worst performing region for pay below the [living wage]. The North East of England is a close second with 24%, but even Wales records a significantly lower figure at 22%. An overall UK figure would be skewed by figures for London, but even without it we can see that Northern Ireland is not above average for low pay it is top of the table. (27)

There have been significant declines, for example, in manufacturing from 12.3% to 11.5% and, not surprisingly, the biggest fall in employment share was in construction, where the employment share declined from 10.3% to 7.3%. There were small increases in share of employment in agriculture, forestry and fishing – 3.8% to 3.9%. The largest increases in employment share have been in distribution, hotels and restaurants (from 19% to 21.2%), in transport and communication (3.8% to 5.4%), and in banking and finance (10.8% to 11.1%). Mac Flynn concludes that,

> There are trends emerging within the Northern Ireland labour market that pose a series of challenges for policymakers. The pattern of employment has shifted toward particular groups and industries and the shape and form of employment has shifted also. The available evidence suggests that these shifts may result in a growth of low paid and insecure work. The first challenge is to tackle low pay through increased wage floors and to promote wage agreements across sectors. Regulation also needs to ensure that employees cannot be exploited through the use of flexible contracts by introducing minimum work requirements. (32-33)

With this in mind, it is important to remember the TUC (2015) data referred to above which found that the "new precarious job" is one bounded by what it termed "Victorian era" conditions. Moreover, "Too often workers on such contracts face working conditions better suited to the Victorian era than 21st century Britain" (TUC 2015, 3). Mac Flynn's analysis complements the TUC's 2015 report, based on aggregate UK data. The TUC report states that,

> Those employed in precarious jobs tend not only to experience heightened job insecurity but also a significant pay penalty. Most have seen no benefits from the recovery.

Instead they often find it difficult to make ends meet, with some resorting to pay day loans or even food banks to cover basic household bills and feed their families.

But job insecurity in the UK is not limited to low-paid, low-skilled employment. Levels of insecurity are also rising amongst higher skilled and better paid staff working in professional occupations including education, health care and the entertainment sector. University lecturers, radiographers and even airline pilots have all been affected by the employer drive towards more flexible and insecure forms of work. The unpredictability of their take home pay makes it increasingly difficult for individuals and households to plan financially, to access credit, and to secure mortgages or tenancy agreements. Constantly varying working hours also has an impact on family life, making it difficult for individuals to organise childcare, the care of older relatives and a social life. (TUC 2015, 3)

According to the JRF (2016), employment growth remains feeble throughout the UK:

- Northern Ireland has not experienced the same strong employment performance as Great Britain, only now reaching pre-recession levels. Since 2011, the working-age employment rate has increased by 0.6 percentage points, compared with a 3.0 percentage point increase in GB.

- The overall employment rate in NI is five percentage points lower than in GB. For some groups, the gap is much wider – 15 percentage points lower for disabled people in NI compared with GB, 12 each for lone parents and 16-24 year olds.

- Average weekly pay is lower in Northern Ireland than a decade ago (after inflation). The gap with GB has remained steady at the median, but low-paid workers have fallen further behind those in GB. (Tinson and MacInnes 2016)

So if we had to draw a broad picture of the political economy in the North, it would be one characterised by an abundance of the worst aspects of neo-liberal labour markets with its consequent pattern of social and economic subordinations and exclusions: low pay, temporary jobs in sectors continuing to display well-known, historical, characteristics of weak labour protections including the usual picture of weak or non-existent trade unions. Given what we know of the outworking of neo-liberalism and the typically negative ways in which it is being played out in the UK as a whole, we can see also that the North represents an economy in an even worse state of disrepair. In terms of work and employment in the North, there are relatively more people experiencing "Victorian era" working conditions, while (unsurprisingly) registering higher levels of poverty.

So, poverty is fundamentally central to this economy: poor jobs, poor housing and poor democratic representation are inextricably bound together. We will deal with the latter in our concluding chapter but for the moment we reflect on the way poverty defines the life experiences and opportunities of so many people in the North of Ireland. Focusing on "poverty, work and education", according to the JRF,

- Twenty per cent of people in Northern Ireland (NI) were in poverty after housing costs on average in the two years to 2013/14. This is around the same as Great Britain and a little higher than before the recession.

- The composition of those in poverty in Northern Ireland has changed over the last five years. There are more working-age adults, particularly young people, more private renters and fewer pensioners in poverty.

- Around 60 per cent of boys and 50 per cent of girls eligible for free school meals do not get five good GCSEs, compared with 30 per cent and 20 per cent of those not eligible. Pupils receiving free school meals do less well than other pupils in non-grammar schools and slightly less well in grammar schools. (Tinson and MacInnes 2016)

And lest it be assumed that poverty is a lifelong experience only for those born into the host community, data from a range of sources highlights its impact on migrant communities. Barnardo's NI (McGovern et al. 2011) and the Joseph Rowntree Foundation (Wallace et al. 2103) highlighted the resource problems attending migrant families in the north while over a decade ago McAliskey et al. (2006) reported on the difficulties families faced accessing basic social and other services. This remains the case today for many. The JRF report by Olivia Lucas and Neil Jarman, *Poverty and Ethnicity: Key Messages for Northern Ireland* (2016), has specifically called for recognition of the very particular problems faced by new and longer-standing migrants and their families. These include difficulties in accessing social and governmental agencies (essentially, health and housing amenities), "inequality and segregation in the employment market" (Lucas and Jarman 2016, 3), and racist attitudes. And in case a liberal agenda can take comfort in various polices addressing discrimination against new and older arrivals here, they might think again about the relative absence of challenges to racism directed towards our own indigenous communities and notably the traveller community. Travellers "continue to suffer from particularly severe inequalities in the areas of employment, education, accommodation and health" (3).

And so, in understanding the rise of the new, neo-liberal North, we feel it is necessary to reflect the experiences of many who have come to the North in recent years. Migration has always been our experience, or at least a form of migration has prevailed for people and their families here. What is different is that since 2004, there has been reverse migration: for the first time in centuries, inward migration has exceeded outward migration. To say something of this we turn to work by the Migrant Action Research Network (MARN), whose activities since 2012 have sought to chart migrant experiences of the North, including arriving, working and living here, and raising families. MARN has operated on the basis that while recognising the crucial work of both mainstream democratic organisations such as trade unions and NGOs, a critical perspective also requires channels to migrant communities lying outside mainstream channels and networks while accepting degrees of overlap. For example, a number of those involved in MARN were, and remain, members of mainstream NGOs and trade unions. It is to the experiences and testimonies of those engaged in MARN, contextualised in relation to what some see as the peculiarities of Northern society, to which we now turn (Garvey et al. 2010).

In Chapter 1 we emphasised the way in which neo-liberalism had taken root in the north in ways quite distinctive to the UK. While undermining manufacturing and developing a dependant service economy as could be witnessed in the rise of FIRE (McCabe), significant elements of Keynesian welfare state institutions and practices deemed essential to maintain the peace were not only preserved but given a new lease of life. This was the context in which thousands of new migrants came to the North after 2004.

Migrant workers and the north of Ireland[4]

Coming to the north of Ireland and low
paid and precarious work

For more than eighty years labour market migration was predominantly that of emigration from the north of Ireland to elsewhere in the UK and Britain's other former colonies. The period of conflict lasting thirty-five years entrenched a remarkable lack of ethnic diversity; an economy comprising labour markets and political-spatial relationships premised upon sociopolitical divisions around two central, determinate confessional identities and habitation boundaries (McVeigh, 2007; Maguire, 1988; Shirlow and Murtagh, 2006). This is crucial to understanding migrant worker experiences at work, home and in the community. After the 2004 European enlargement the local labour market expanded with the arrival of 21–25,000 migrants from the new EU countries, many of whom found employment in low-wage, unregulated sectors. The concentration of migrant workers in low-skill-low-wage jobs outside the public sector, despite their relatively high levels of education, is consistent with findings across the UK (Office for National Statistics (ONS) and Department of Trade, Enterprise and Investment (DETI), 2009). They have been seeking employment in a society where since 2008 significant public sector retrenchment has seen cuts to a range of local community, post-conflict-resolution programmes accounting for the employment of up to 10,000 workers. Set against this background, it is not always obvious what is specific about the experience of

---

4   The section titled "Migrant workers and the north of Ireland" and the "Discussion and conclusion" section that follows it have been reproduced here with kind permission from Garvey, B., and Stewart, P., (2015) *Work, Employment and Society*. Vol. 29(3) 392-408.

migration to the North. As Wilhelmas (Lithuania) suggests, "I remember I was working 120 hours in one week, and 44 hours non-stop, non-stop! It was like, work, home, sleep, work, home, sleep." And Inga's (Lithuania) experience testifies to the "exploitation" and "unconditional" offer of employment facing new migrants in many cases in the North and elsewhere in the British Isles: "We were told we had to sign a form if we wanted to work here."

As in many other places, agencies, whether recruiting in the worker's country of origin or locally in the North, are a major factor in the migrant's experience:

My first job was through an agency, in Armagh and Dungannon, anywhere. [...] But [...my] agency boss told me I can't go because there was some small writing in my contract with the agency that when I finish the work then the company must pay the agency some money for me, because of something I had signed ... I didn't have translator when I signed this [...]. Now I'm Bank staff but we don't have contract hours [...]. I get holiday pay based on the hours of work, but I don't know if I get maternity pay. (Paulena, Poland)

This febrile situation was a common experience for many new migrant workers, revealing a context of insecurity: labour contract precarity and bullying and racist labour conditions:

I hear people complaining Black people are taking "our jobs" [...] when I came here there were jobs that local people did not want to do like cleaning, care assistants. [...] I used to work in "I" cleaning company but I left because the girl I worked with was very abusive, she used to say "you come to work here and you think this is your country, this is not your country". (Sherley, Liberia)

While these accounts provide us with insight into initial experiences of "coming here" to work in low-paid occupations, employment, though an encounter involving broader aspects of acceptance, struggle and mutual support, can also involve isolation. As Marta (Poland) put it, "At work no one talks to us. It's hard to get information. When I came [...] I didn't know how to do better, today I still don't know, nobody wants to tell you."

Community and social life

In the north of Ireland, already existing sectarianism gives the experience of migration an added piquancy. This sectarianism underpins, at the same time as it refracts, experiences in determinate ways, but it is most obviously witnessed in the polarisation of living areas and social spaces that are a well-documented consequence of recent conflict (inter alia Shirlow and Murtagh, 2006) while of course predating the long insurgency. In the "post-conflict" period (post-1998 GFA) this social rigidity has been sustained through reinforcing sectarian parochialism and territoriality:

> I heard yesterday a man got shot in Belfast but I think the situation is getting *better* between Catholics and Protestants ... but I was going to _____ bar, all Catholics at work were saying "oh don't go there, it's so dangerous". (Jovita, Poland)

Jovita's testimony points to the noise of political and community discourses that have focused on the war between two dominant communities drowning out a diversity of experience that includes hostility to migrant workers, domestic and sexual violence (see especially Jarman, 2006; Women's Aid Federation NI, 2010). Raul from Brazil was frustrated by the limiting nature of debate in the North:

> You see when people here talk about "community" [...] it doesn't matter if they're loyalists, or people calling themselves

Republican socialists, when they talk about my community it's Catholic, Irish, Nationalist, or British and Protestant. It leaves no room for me.

As if to reinforce this, Andrius recounted how a group of young people who, when challenged by the local community leaders (who are paramilitaries) about their assault on Lithuanians, claimed, "We thought we were doing our community a favour." At work, this exclusion was perceived in typically racist terms and was experienced by a high percentage of focus group members. As Kin (Nigeria) reflected,

> There are workplaces if you are Black they don't want to talk to you, they don't want to share things with you, they want you to get mad [...] to provoke you the way they look at you, [...] but if you are not strong enough they can push you to the wall.

While again this highlights the particular form of the porosity of work–life boundaries in the North, perhaps Gedi (Lithuania) and Rosa (Spain), provide exemplary testimony:

> This thing with Catholics and Protestants here is ridiculous. (Gedi)

> Yeah, politics here are around the same topic. [...] They've made them to be too interested in the Catholic and Protestant thing, they don't think about socialism, workers or the green movement, they are too concentrated in the Irish–British thing. When I first moved here I thought that people were very conscious of politics, because they are all day talking about it, but in the end after a while I just realized that people [...] just see what there was back in the past, they're still isolated: if you were born in a certain area you stay in a certain circle of people, they don't see any further. (Rosa)

The "isolation", parochialism and polarisation of social life that are observed by participants make it difficult to initiate or sustain friendships within or outside of work:

> The Irish, they are forcing us into our own corners, which is really bad. (Kin)

> You see if you didn't go to school with them, grow up with them, it's hard to get to know them. (Sherley)

This, as will be seen, has obvious consequences for attempts by migrant workers to reform their workplaces.

Individual or collective strategies of resilience or resistance

The research suggests that migrant workers are far from passive since in a number of sectors they are actively engaged in protecting labour rights and fighting iniquitous employment conditions. For example:

> I was a member of trade union in Poland – Solidarność. But I wasn't active. Here, life taught me to be active. We had enough of our manager. We knew what was going on and that somewhere wages were better or conditions were better. I am shop steward here. (Joanna, Poland)

And for Gosia (Poland),

> There was no union at work. Nobody had contracts but we joined the union. The manager heard some people had joined and shouted and said he would find out who had joined. But after some time we told him we wanted contracts and now everything is much better [...]. We didn't lose our jobs. People shouldn't be afraid. We got contracts for [...] even the Irish, everyone, for almost 200 people.

These positive accounts are tempered by the frustrations of other workers. Finding themselves isolated at work or undermined by workplace segregation, migrant workers offer a telling critique of society in the North, revealing one aspect of limits to practical workplace resistance in a sectarian society. This is important because despite the nature of the North's otherwise highly politicised "equalities rights" culture there remain gaps more usually served by sectarian politics. One significant case from the fieldwork exemplifies the relationship between "typical" managerial paternalism, worker competition and the new form of sectarianism whose character was described above. This complexity presents further problems for migrant workers fighting for better conditions, and what makes it especially notable is that for many participants, it is local workers who have eroded workplace protection, leaving many migrants exposed to unfair treatment.

Northern-Recycling (Belfast) and Tatties-Now illustrate key features of this complexity. At Northern-Recycling, Lithuanian workers in dispute found that unionisation and improved conditions were being undermined by local workers (who maintained separate indigenous–migrant respite rooms). In highlighting victimisation as a result of a fight for improved conditions one of the migrants argued that, "Only Lithuanian guys at work will support me ... the others [indigenous] – no chance" (Vaidas).

This subordination – divide and rule – was highlighted when a Lithuanian worker attempting to ask an Irish colleague where he kept his mobile phone (after Lithuanian workers had been told they must keep theirs in their cars) was instructed "forcefully" by the manager that he was not to ask any questions of other staff. The effect of this oppressive managerial approach combined with an absence of any workplace solidarity from co-native workers soon became evident. After workers were informed that working hours were to be reduced when the company allegedly lost a contract, the union advised one Lithuanian worker to ask the employer about the status of the contract, as it appeared there had been no reduction in waste coming through the company. He laughed, "No chance, if we can't ask a co-worker where he keeps his phone, how are we going to question management?" Nevertheless, they continued with an internal grievance, protesting at two unfair dismissals. Threats made beyond the workplace were followed by attacks on two workers' property. In the end the workers deemed it safer to withdraw from work than continue to challenge the unjust treatment.

The significance of migrant-led union organisation in spite of indigenous worker passivity, or indeed hostility, was reinforced by Lynne (Lithuania) in Tatties-Now, a food processing plant:

> At 11am the machines were stopped, all staff called to the central floor as the manager brandished a union form. He told staff he would find out who was behind this, threatened them that the company had its own solicitors and it was illegal to join a union if you had not worked for two years or more in the plant.

Nonetheless, the Lithuanian workers raised a collective grievance and gained written contracts for everyone, significantly reducing supervisor bullying while obtaining health and safety assurances. Despite the relatively large workforce (almost ninety) that included a number of native workers, contact between foreign and locally born staff remains limited. Arguably this nativist depoliticisation is sustained by a wider culture of depoliticisation alluded to by Rosa (above).

Indeed, despite the optimism presented in many of these testimonies, the difficulty of forging workplace cooperation-cum-solidarities is a common theme and friendships at work, like those outside are described more often as "superficial" and difficult to sustain. This has the effect of leaving many workers in this research to reflect on the larger social structural peculiarities of the North and their impact on work, social and family life. Many realise that while they are confronting a range of subordinations at work (place) and in space (hierarchy), some of which are not uncommon to those experienced by migrants in other jurisdictions, in the North, the nature of the society riven by pre-existing forms of social subordination is sometimes made worse by the new political settlement: the political settlement (GFA) is of course also a social settlement. This settlement is allowing the main protagonists to the older conflict time to divide the spoils – the "price of peace" – and as such often leaves new entrants exposed in myriad ways, but especially in those small and medium-sized enterprises (SMEs) controlled by ex-combatants whose reproduction of former *sectarian alliances* between management and workers is tolerated to the disadvantage of those outside the "hallowed ground" of the North's older sociopolitical divide. Northern-Recycling was owned by, and its core (native-born) workers came from, one section of the community. What is more, at the community level, where people live, the GFA has continued to reproduce relatively static spaces of habitation in which outsiders are often deemed a threat. As Shirlow and Murtagh (2006) have demonstrated, Protestants and Catholics continue to live where they always lived (more or less) and incomers must accommodate to this (more or less). In addition, migrants will find that their often less desirable accommodation will dovetail with their lower status in job hierarchies lying outside already existing and often intergenerational and sectarian friendship networks.

So while it is important to identify the *places* where migrants work, it is nevertheless the case that where they are positioned *in* these "places" matters: "migrants ... are immediately identifiable. As a group they are at the bottom of every scale; wages, type of work; job security, housing, education, purchasing power" (Berger and Mohr, 1975: 143). Thus one finds that where indigenous workers were present alongside migrant workers in low-paid occupations, often the division of labour extends to a hierarchy of roles within the workplace, as was expressed by Dan, from Romania:

> I worked through an agency, in the big supermarkets. The Irish workers were full-time staff. The agency workers were Russian, Polish, Romanian, Brazilian and it was okay, but we did the heavy work and nights.

Kristina from Poland (care home agency worker) also perceived that local workers in the same occupational space seemed to be offered preferential working patterns:

> This boy from Romania, he was given shifts that I don't think a local worker would be asked to do, and a Chinese girl, she was asked to work from 9pm to 11pm then 8am till late the next day.

Yet the fact of a workplace migrant division of labour in which migrants are put in their place (where they work) and space (hierarchy) tied to extra-work community associations needs to be continually highlighted. In other words, this is where workplace subordination meets subordination beyond work. [We now assess] a number of potential sociopolitical reasons accounting for what could be interpreted as the paradox of migrant experience in the North. On the one hand experiences are often seen as unexceptional in comparison with migrant experiences elsewhere, while on the other the distinctiveness of the North soon becomes apparent. The research suggests the latter results from the confrontation between the 1998 settlement and its outworking in the context of deregulated neo-liberal environments in which this taken-for-granted "new" order is challenged (if not overtly) by workers otherwise marginal to the peace settlement.

Discussion and conclusion

This research sought to address two perceived underdevelopments in recent migration literature. First, by considering the role of sectarianism in the context of new patterns of globalisation (specifically neo-liberalism), the study addressed a number of aspects of the ways in which migrant experiences are affected by pre-existing social constructions. Second, and relatedly, the research explored a number of ways in which local resistance to integration recreated established patterns of paternalistic exclusion. In order to investigate these related processes, we have considered the degree to which sectarian labour markets and spatial-living segregation in the North impact upon migrants in ways distinctive from those experienced by long-term residents. The research found limited support for the thesis that exclusionary, including racist, responses to migrants in work vary significantly from those experienced by migrants settling in other parts of the British Isles. That said, racism in the north of Ireland is made more complex by the historical role of sectarianism. Itself a determinate form of racism, sectarianism was, in its original incarnation, a state and economic strategy of social and political subordination of one section of the community by the other. Sectarian subordination furthers inter-communal conflict and as a consequence inevitably links to work and employment in historically informed ways. These links are important in allowing us to better illustrate the extent to which what goes on *in* work, how people interpret their work, is also an effect of what goes on *beyond* workplace boundaries.

Under the auspices of the GFA sectarianism has, paradoxically, acquired an added dimension where it has been reborn as a form of legitimated state brokerage. It is a paradox because while society is committed to prosecuting sectarian attacks, state disbursement of the GFA largesse reinforces the structural pillars of the old sectarian society dominated by two key community identities: Unionism and Nationalism. The growing strength of sectarian ideology and culture is perhaps nowhere more evident than in the proliferation of so-called Peace Walls (four in 1998 compared to more than fifty in 2013). The original state strategy driving the 1998 settlement leaned towards social democratic socio-economic stability measures. Since the onset of the economic crisis and since the formation of the UK's ConDem government in 2010, Stormont's strategy has been more determinedly neo-liberal, with the assumption that expansion in newly state-privatised and other private sectors of the economy would not compromise the 1998 settlement. The research unearthed one possibly overlooked feature of the GFA: attempts to keep the older (sectarian) divide in aspic have, under the pressure of neo-liberal globalisation, exposed another dimension of dysfunctionality. The sociopolitical inflexibility of the older taken-for-granted "peace-settlement-sectarianism" is now rubbing up against the newly deregulated neo-liberal economy. This social structural dysfunctionality is to be seen in certain SMEs where ex-combatants, given permissive tolerance as a result of the new dispensation, depend upon older sectarian cross-class paternalism to maintain order in the employment relationship, free from the restraint of trade unionism (let alone contemporary new management protocol). Illegal threats and occasional violent chastisement are on occasion used to resolve labour–management disputes, as was seen at Northern-Recycling.

The case of Northern-Recycling is significant since it highlights a number of latent features of the impact of sectarian social relations upon employment norms in particular settings including both existing and "new" communities and wider political society. First, since the North has now politically institutionalised sectarianism it is argued that this impacts upon new entrants' participation in political society both locally and in the Assembly: one can be Polish or Lithuanian, but one must also either be an Irish Nationalist or an Ulster Unionist according to Assembly voting protocol. Second, migrants' subordination in weakly regulated sectors is impacted by the fact that the state and trade unions, while more comfortable with conventional contests in the public sector, by and large are tolerant, often standing aside, in disputes in sectors controlled by former combatants when conflicts should be seen as traditional labour disputes. In these and some other SMEs, migrant labour is particularly prevalent. While one might argue this is an egregious example, it is nevertheless significant in that it highlights the tensions and some of the reality behind the veil of the "North-as-normal". Of course, not all migrant workers work in SMEs and not all SMEs operate in the shadowland of unreconstructed sectarian paternalism. However, making sense of SMEs' impact upon migrant workers allows a degree of insight into another aspect of the growing tension between regulated Keynesianism to end the conflict and the advance of contemporary neo-liberal state strategies. This research, while demonstrating some commonality with migrant experiences elsewhere, also brings out a variant of subordination distinctive to the north of Ireland.

Migrant workers coming to the north of Ireland typically find themselves in the midst of a polarised environment not of their choosing. Initial optimistic narratives were on occasion displaced by other feelings of unease and the sense that the North is indeed a difficult place for migrants

(Sherley, Liberia, and Kin, Nigeria). While that initial sense of the North-as-normal could sustain the conclusions of other research, the methodology establishing extended relationships with the project research participants allowed the exploration of a range of other perspectives. Among these was the realisation that the North, though in many respects accepting of new workers, was also hamstrung by already existing exclusionary sociocultural realities (Vaidas, Northern-Recycling). These realities encompass community associations (where one can feel comfortable) and perceptions of who "we" are, and they reach into workplace affiliations and identities. The signally important reality is that of sectarian socio-economic relationships embracing people whether at home, in communities or at work. These historical patterns have been sustained by the institutional development of a sanctioned political class constituted by the outworking of the 1998 GFA. This class has a contradictory place in the communities out of which it emerged for while it is sustained by them, in line with the dominant discourse about the "North", this political class interprets other social and ethnic tensions as secondary to the key binary divide of Protestant/Catholic–Irish Nationalist/Unionist (Rosa).

A significant issue is that new workers introduce other narratives into and about communities and workplaces not readily constituted by the sectarian binary divide in and beyond work. Again, a challenge to the dominant story of the singular binary divide in the North was witnessed at Northern-Recycling. An otherwise conventional labour struggle initiated by migrant workers highlighted a new, unforeseen development: a latent tension between the Keynesian GFA's division-of-spoils between the two dominant social groups and state-sanctioned neo-liberalism. In some SME sectors neo-liberalism is blind to the continuation of older sectarian tropes of subordination supposedly prohibited by the GFA, concerned as the latter inevitably is, with the disbursement of resources to public- and state-selected actors. This has allowed the state and some union centres often to turn a blind eye to the activities of some former sectarians, less concerned in their SMEs, by forms of state regulation of the employment relationship. The manifest labour challenge to Northern-Recycling's management interestingly revealed a structural accommodation between the Keynesian GFA and neo-liberal development wherein competition, so carefully managed within the state sector by management and unions, was determined by ex-combatants. While the home-grown labour force had been prepared largely to accept their paternalistic employment conditions, temporary migrant workers, less conditioned (since they were excluded) by the older sectarian paternalism, saw their relationship to management in conventional employment terms. Northern-Recycling revealed that the experiences of some migrant workers result from the structural accommodation of the new sectarian dispensation to neo-liberalism. Finally, and relatedly, the notion of community too proved to be somewhat more problematical than the often emollient association with positive integration (for a critique see Holgate et al., 2012, and of course, Coates and Silburn's (1973) classic community study set in working-class Nottingham). In communities in the north of Ireland, competition for "place" can be exclusivist and subordinating not least for new entrants. The latter also may be faced with long-term residents whose sense of place is being renewed in the face of perceived challenges from those beyond "their" communities. In such instances, the sometimes violent exercise of territorial power must be constantly negotiated by newcomers.

Chapter 3

Unionism-Loyalism and the New Sectarian State

Our argument about Tuaisceart Éireann Nua, the "new" Northern Ireland (with apologies, a fraction of the one-time sought-for holy grail of Eire Nua!), has been that the new state, the Northern Ireland Assembly, extended, while moderating, key features of the old Orange state. Specifically, while the sectarian Orange state was characterised by the dominance of the cross-class Protestant alliance wherein Protestant workers rested mostly quietly at the bottom of a heap, nevertheless, their heap rested on top of another heap comprising (as was intended) most though certainly not all of the Catholic community. We write "most" because Orange sectarianism did not preclude space for a small and politically marginalised Catholic middle class, as is well known and which we have highlighted elsewhere (McKearney 2011) in the context of the story now being developed here.

In this chapter we argue that the more usual way to understand Loyalism – which is to see it as a working-class ideology attached to street, and in many other instances paramilitary, activity – is in some respects to misinterpret its real significance. While these descriptions of what so-called Loyalists do are often accurate, confining the description to guns/no guns – streets/parliament is to underestimate its significance. We argue the best place to start is with a historically grounded analysis that relates the rise of so-called Loyalism to the fate of the Orange state and, following its demise, of the new Sectarian State. Thus, we reject the too easy class and political-ideological distinction between Unionism and Loyalism (for an example of this approach which we reject see McAuley 2015) arguing that understanding the rise and nature of Loyalism has to be related to the practices of the state of Northern Ireland as defined by the GFA of 1998. Loyalism is not the creation of the Northern Ireland state but rather the form taken by Unionism where the state is premised on sustaining sectarian division – this part of civil society and the state for the Catholic community, that part of the state for the Protestant community.

The new sectarian state and understanding Unionism-Loyalism

One of the great shape-shifting features of the new sectarian state has been to make it seem as if now we have a secular society: since both communities are supposedly beneficiaries, at least no one comes out on top any more. The horrible word "sectarianism" has been abandoned in official discourse. The hope is that people will think that because both sides are treated the same sectarianism no longer holds sway at the level of officialdom and the state more broadly. Everyone can be certain of this. Equivalence of certainty at least in relative plenitude, or is it servitude? As we have argued in Chapter 1, the demise of post-war social democracy, witnessed daily in the continuing privatisation and marketisation of the Keynesian welfare state, has left fewer and fewer pickings for everyone not reliant on a vibrant private sector economy, which means fewer than before 1998 certainly (Garvey and Stewart 2015). The deepening attacks on public sector finances have, it goes without too much shouting about the obvious, intensified the fight over what remains in the welfare and wider public sector budget. The implications of financialisation, central to the development of contemporary globalisation (neo-liberal capitalism) for community organisations, many of which became, rightly, spaces for reform, or at least, reconsideration by many of the older sectarian values since 1998, are becoming profoundly negative.

This increasing attack on the public purse is thus another factor to be taken into account, bearing in mind our view that the GFA "peace settlement" has been hamstrung from the start. Though the GFA was feeble to start with, the shocking story of its compromise is also one of *the* stories of the retrenchment of a repressive state and society. The new sectarian state is certainly built upon a shared understanding that the state's (dwindling) largesse can now be dispensed "equally" across the two communities such that community leaders, political parties from both sides of the sectarian divide, will be the adjudicators of the claims to funding. Yet the sectarian dispensation sustaining, promoting this, has accordingly continued and at the same time advanced some of the worst features of the former Orange sectarian state. Why do we argue this? How can this be allowed when even the weariest participants fall back on epithets such as, one of our favourites, "At least we have a quiet life now where everyone can go about their lawful business." Or, what about, "Well at least everyone is happy now that they get equal access to a share of the pie," and even better, "At least the killing has stopped."

Yet, these platitudes mask a deepening malaise which we attribute to the ossification of sectarian social relationships within and, in several instances, between the dominant communities. Moreover, our argument is that this conflict, this malaise, where not only have things not improved from a civil society standpoint but in critical instances have actually deteriorated, is directly attributable to the character of the "new" state as it developed in the run-up to, and in the outworking of, the GFA. With regards to the specific working of what was the Northern Ireland (Orange) state in the context of institutional reform (the D'Hondt Principles), we have elaborated on this above (see too, Garvey and Stewart 2015). In this chapter, we want to explore the critical, though sometimes sympathetic, ways in which one side of the sectarian divide has been understood. The chapter highlights both the relatively stable nature of sectarian politics and also the fact that one of the key factors in the way sectarian politics play out in both Irish Nationalist and Unionist-Loyalist communities is both state-dependent and state driven. This is another of way of saying that while in this instance Unionism-Loyalism comprises aspects that remain undiminished and in some instances with features predating Partition, the way in which these play out is always context and conjuncture specific.

In linking what many commentators more usually see as distinct political views and approaches taken by those in Northern Ireland committed to the connection with Britain, Unionist *or* Loyalist, we argue that this division is sometimes misunderstood. Seeing Unionism and Loyalism as almost different beliefs, or ideologies, offers particular advantages for those comfortable with the distinction as a means to differentiate between the main currents within Unionism. Arguing that there is an inherent strategic and sociocultural difference between Unionism and Loyalism allows, and therefore perpetuates, what we see as an abiding myth. This myth works to sanitise those who pursue a liberal democratic agenda as Unionists – the nice, clean, middle-class people in the Assembly – while stigmatising those who fight for the same goals on the streets – the dirty unwashed working class from the Shankill, Rathcoole, East Belfast, the Fountain in Derry, and elsewhere. The media finds the division colourful, especially when it comes to the aspects of so-called "Loyalist" culture, from marches (and marching bands) to the Flag Protest. This is important to continually feed the myth of division between safe-middle-class-Unionist/dangerous-working-class-Loyalist. Very neat, until the neat clear-cut division begins to break down both conceptually and in practice.

Conceptually, dividing pro-British sentiment in this way is to misread recent history. This in turn can only be the result of a misreading of the history of the old Orange state and especially what are referred to as its repressive apparatuses – the regular RUC and its parastate auxiliaries, principally the B-Specials, were always, and with good reason, institutionally part of the Orange state and were constituted prior to the state's formation in 1920: indeed, without them, as we know, the state could neither have been created nor lasted for very long. But these repressive apparatuses were not simply posted from on high by the remnants of the old Irish Unionist Alliance for they depended upon mobilisation from a section of the labour movement in the northern counties of Ireland. The strongest support for a British-centred trade unionism was to be found amongst a large number of shipyard workers in Belfast. A not insignificant number of them were mobilised by Carson and Andrews in 1918 when the latter set up the Ulster Unionist Labour Association (UULA). The UULA provided the backbone to a vigilante group which acted in turn as a parastate militia in the run-up to the creation of the Northern Ireland state. In turn, inevitably, it was brought together with the UVF to form the basis for the B-Specials (Bew, Gibbon and Patterson 2002, 18-19). Thus, in the good old days (about which we have written elsewhere and to which we allude only briefly herein) state security was perpetuated by full-time and part-time employment for workers, mostly from the politically and demographically dominant Protestant community.

A number of accounts, from academics and other commentators particularly in the mainstream media, on occasion confuse the nature of the divisions within communities committed to maintaining the British link (McAuley 2015). The account, for example by James McAuley, of the defining features of Loyalism in contrast to Unionism, lacks sociological substance where what he terms "ontological" differences are not ontological differences at all (3-7). When it's the working class in Protestant areas, Unionists who take to the streets are described as Loyalists: it's the Prods in the streets, the plebs; the terrifying masses. What McAuley is talking about is Unionist politics in Protestant working-class neighbourhoods.

This is fine and we can understand the point he is trying to make. However, in trying to draw a definitional line between Loyalism and Unionism the account disappears into a series of vignettes of Protestant working-class pro-UK politics on the Shankill or in East Belfast. This is usually defined by reference to activities such as Orange parades, flag protests and paramilitary actions and membership. It is true that most Unionists from the wealthier parts of the north are less likely to demonstrate on the streets, join paramilitary organisations or play in Orange bands: "most" we write, although it's reasonable to assume more than a few went to Protestant grammar schools. However, it does not describe difference in the form of pro-UK commitments just because Unionists in different places are interested in a variety of forms of Unionist-Loyalist activity.

The point, as we argue throughout, is that just because some are Unionists in Parliament while some are Unionists on the streets it does not follow that the substance of what they speak to is different, which is what McAuley is arguing. It is obvious indeed from his book's title, *Very British Rebels?*, that in his attempt to find differences between those he terms Loyalists, as against those described as Unionists, that actual, material differences are not existent. In his attempt to describe "Unionist" beliefs as in some sense different to "loyalist" cultural-political differences we find no differences at all. Instead what we are presented with is the following: when it's the Protestant working class it's Loyalism and when commitment to Britain is middle class it's Unionism. So it's really a story about class differences in the fight to maintain the link with Britain. The rest – notions about ethnocultural and historical differences – are inventions, inventions by sectarians. They are inventions, key myths that McAuley falls into the trap of interpreting as real political-ideological differences defining the non-existent divide between Unionists and Loyalists. This does not mean that we do not recognise the differences between the ideas of Unionism and Loyalism. As we argue, they are significant enough but not in the way that some might argue and certainly not in the way described by McAuley.

This matters and of course there is a difference between "Loyalism" and "Unionism", just as there is a difference between those committed to a united Ireland one would term Nationalists as opposed to those described as Republicans. However, in the case of a British-centred commitment, the loyalty is no less loyal on the Malone Road than on the Newtownards Road, the Shankill or Rathcoole, whereas the distinctions between (Irish) Nationalists and Irish republicans are often profoundly distinct at the levels not just of means but of ends. Nevertheless, the point of distinguishing between Loyalism and Unionism is to suggest that the former lead *and led* tainted, "criminal" or potentially criminal lives, which is how the establishment supposedly looks at the street fighters of Unionism.

Today Unionism, in the media in particular, likes to treat its boys (and sometimes) girls on the streets with class condescension and disdain. But as we know it was not always thus and certainly not even in recent times. Moreover, we know that the differences between those described as Loyalists and those described as Unionists can quickly blur: Big House Unionists and Peter Robinson's other house Unionists, several hundred in total, found easy common cause in their gun attack on a poor field in the border town of Clontibret in County Monaghan in 1986. Robinson had led the "Ulster Resistance" movement formed in November of that year. Nor was Trimble's rapprochement with the Reverend Ian Paisley, and so-called street-fighting

Loyalists, when they sallied forth on the Garvachy Road, inhibited by the different class backgrounds of the various protagonists. In reality, and for the most part after 1968, the purpose of the distinction was to sanitise pro-British political attitudes so that the commitment to Britain, in so far as this was advanced by means of parliamentary politics, could be seen as beyond reproach. This approach would especially be pursued by the nice ones – our Unionists – leaving the nasty ones – our Loyalists – to fight in the street: or today to wave the flag.

We may forgive the wag who thought that this largely spurious way to distinguish between the main forces within Unionism would allow us now to describe pro-British political formations as comprising those who would fight to maintain British rule with Stormont notepaper in one hand and a Rangers flag in the other. This is another way of saying that while the distinction between Unionism and Loyalism matters, it is spurious to draw the main fault line as between those who want to maintain the Union with Britain by fighting in Stormont and local councils (the nice middle classes) and those who are more readily content to use direct action (the not always so nice Protestant working class).

As we will argue, this is about strategy and tactics and not about "Unionist" principles depending upon class difference, though it does not mean class differences are unimportant in the social composition of the UUP/DUP/PUP.[5] But it is important to maintain the difference between Unionism and Loyalism nevertheless for those wanting to argue that we can support any view, that all views are equally worthy of acceptance, depending on their attitude to violence/non-violence. Or that this is even a useful way historically to understand the character of Unionism and its attitude to parliamentary/non-parliamentary strategies.

5   Ulster Unionist Party/Democratic Unionist Party/Progressive Unionist Party

Talking about physical, as opposed to psychical, force Unionism misses the point. It also allows for a way to find redemptive features within Loyalism too, since if we can delineate between Loyalists committed to "Stormont notepaper" and those committed to waving a "Rangers flag", never mind a Northern Ireland flag, then we have found a way to distinguish the grown-ups from the delinquents. Peter Shirlow's (2012) interesting research, as we shall see, distinguishes between "regressive" Loyalism ("super Loyalists" following his citation of Gusty Spence, 10; see 11-16) and "transformation-led Loyalism" (16-17): the "bad" Protestant working-class types from the "good" Protestant working-class types. This is also a neat way to say that not only are the Loyalists not all unwashed but that at least, unlike the Unionists of the UUP/DUP, they are not hypocrites. The principle problem with this approach is that it too readily assumes, or lets loose the idea, that Unionism is a middle-class pursuit while Loyalism is a working-class ideological phenomenon. For us, the problem lies with the notion of a "bad" Loyalism. Before pursuing this further, it is worth recalling that the notion of Loyalism as it is commonly understood is in essence linked to the onset of the insurgency in the late sixties. Before this period it had very little ideological currency within Protestant communities. The reasons for this are plain enough.

In the old days of the Orange state the street fighters of the original Ulster Volunteer Force were not so necessary *as an independent force* after Partition because they could be safely cosseted within the state itself in the guise of the A-, B- and C-Specials, not to mention the RUC proper. After 1972, as the Orange state first showed signs of decay, to be replaced eventually by the new sectarian state after 1998, appearances seemed to offer something quite different. The transformation of the B-Specials into the UDR only appeared to be the decommissioning of Unionism's private army (Boulton 1973; McKearney 2011). What was sacrificed along with the uniform and the emblems was the B-Specials' unique space within society, or, should we say, a particular kind of society. Now that Britain was involved directly in the conflict it was deemed to be quite impossible for the older private army to continue as before. The great benefit of the UDR was that it looked like a British regiment right down to its materiel but it remained in fact the B-Specials recast: what had changed was its function, or rather how and to whom it performed its function. Its role was now modified. While the B-Specials had been focused on monitoring and controlling the Catholic community for the Unionist government, the function of the UDR, now that the Orange state was in crisis and the British were directly involved, was to control an insurgency *within* the Catholic community.

Times had indeed changed and now repression would be shared between the UK government (British Army) and the new Unionists-in-uniform – the UDR. Yet while the constituency of, and for, the "new" force had been repainted (all the people of Northern Ireland can join the new force), it was still predominantly the force of Unionism. More than this, we now know that up until the late nineties, a certain current within the state, still focusing on one community especially, had a hidden, not just painted, face (see Stewart and McKearney 2018).

With the GFA and the rise of the new sectarian state, the need for the ever-so-private-not-so-secret Unionist state repressive force has gone. Or, if this is overstating it, maybe what has happened is that the requirement for a high-profile publicly uniformed private army, whether B-Specials or UDR, has now evaporated. This has left a lot of people – who in days gone by would have had the sanction of state authority at one moment to control and spy on, or control and subjugate (different strategies, different political climates) the Catholic population – "underemployed". We are being only slightly ironic. After all, when a former insurgent leader is the Deputy First Minister and another is deeply committed to the Northern Ireland Policing Board the war is definitely over: for those grand members of the new political class that is. But what if you are a working-class Protestant feeling betrayed by the sins of Big House Unionism in the eighties and nineties and now increasingly so by the apostasy of Semi-Detached House Unionism, the DUP? Where is the institutional and political space for those who in the good ole days would have joined the B-Specials or the UDR? We now know of course of the myriad instances in which Loyalist paramilitaries were also UDR members.

This is not a case of reducing Unionists-Loyalists to dupes but rather of explaining the shifting relations and imperatives of the state's repressive apparatuses and those committed to Unionism-Loyalism and the British state and monarchy.

The many cases of collusion now exposed have highlighted the persistence of this shifting boundary between the state and the paramilitary state: the permeable cordon sanitaire between the state and the Unionist-Loyalist non-state combatants (paramilitaries with their lineage running through the old UVF to the B-Specials and the UDR). (For a historically grounded account of the story of state-Unionist-Loyalist collusion see Ian Cobain's indispensable *The History Thieves: Secrets, Lies and the Shaping of a Modern Nation* (2016)). Increasingly since 1998, at a practical level, the only option for those officially demobbed parastate enthusiasts has been the streets and this is where the understanding of the role of Protestant paramilitaries often goes awry. In contrast to Shirlow's work which fairly attempts to deal with the nature of Loyalism head-on, a number of other studies, much of them also containing otherwise sound social science research, in fear of being accused of patronising working-class Protestants-Unionists, avoid any direct critical engagement with the politics of Protestant paramilitaries.

To assume that those who criticise the activities of Protestant paramilitaries from a left perspective are mainly concerned with trivialising the historically established social nature of Protestant non-state combatants as mere dupes, fall guys for the British state, misses the point. First, it ignores the fact that, on the contrary, paramilitaries are precisely well embedded in Unionist-Loyalist traditions because that is where they come from – their origins. Second, following on from this, if they were indeed merely superficial creations, *agent provocateurs*, of the state, then they could easily have been dealt with by those opposed to them. The fact is that they are neither superficial nor are they to be understood as state agents even if it is one of the intentions of the state that they should be. *However, that said, it is also true that on occasions numbers of Unionist-Loyalist paramilitaries have very willingly acted as state agents, as myriad instances documenting collusion demonstrate.* We have not the space to recount in much detail too the long-running sore haunting the PSNI (Police Service Northern Ireland) to this day, compromising leading RUC officers, of the infamous Cushendall shooting of Catholic RUC Sgt Joseph Campbell in February 1977. Campbell was killed by a Protestant paramilitary network of Loyalist para-militaries and the state. Known as the Glenanne gang,[6] the breadth of membership was impressive. Especially important was what it tells us about the political culture and institutional character of the gang which revealed the easy slippage (network of affiliation) between certain sections of the British state, Northern Ireland's sectarian state and Unionist-Loyalists wedded to traditional beliefs about how to fight to maintain the relationship between the UK and the north. (The fact of its unresolved character is demonstrated by the fate of the Historical

6   The gang, which operated mainly in Armagh and Tyrone, was responsible for bombings and other attacks on Catholics within various communities in the north during the 1970s.

Enquiries Team, including the question of how far up the RUC chain of command knowledge of the gang ran.) The gang comprised members of the UDR, the British Army and the mid-Ulster Brigade of the UVF. The gang had up to two dozen RUC men and British Army members.

Traditionally, when writers and researchers consider the UDA and the UVF or the LVF, the cloud of false class consciousness fogs up a fair treatment of the origins of their politics. Often the central question of the role of these organisations in the context of the new sectarian state is avoided since it is thought that to make direct strategic links between Loyalism and the state reduces their role and activities to mere pawns of state power. To this way of thinking, assuming links between the state and Loyalism merely condescendingly trivialises its whole existence (see our point above regarding collusion). Thus, a proper understanding of Protestant paramilitaries is seen to require a descriptive account that tells us what key figures do and say on issues from policing and paramilitarism-armed struggle, to housing policy, relationships to the Sinn Féin and the wider Republican movement, and the sense of historical betrayal by Big House, or any other house, Unionism. The reports of the UDA seeking a non-violent resolution to a range of issues are impressive, including the *Conflict Transformation Initiative: Loyalism in Transition* agenda set out by the Ulster Political Research Group (2006, cited in Shirlow, 151-54; CTI document is held by Peter Shirlow) and the work of the UVF on the Shankill to present a cross-sectarian story (using murals with English and Irish) about the role of Catholics in the British Army and notably the Somme in the First World War. These are indeed impressive, and notably the objective of presenting the latter as an exemplar of a "peoples' history" (Shirlow, 163) is a salutary reminder of the incorporation of the working-class suffering in wars by the political and cultural elites.

This is very important but then we have to also remind ourselves that the story the Shankill murals want to tell is not just about the fact that Protestants *and* Catholics fought at the Somme, and that this shows that they, Catholics, have been hidden from history, but that we all need reminding that Catholics too fought for King and Country. Furthermore, that they, like their Protestant counterparts, were in fact fellow countrymen who were betrayed by Britain – just like Protestant workers. Betrayed by Britain and the ruling class but also possibly, betrayed by Republicans who have denied, so this narrative goes, the role of Catholics in the British Army, fighting for the British state in the First World War (ibid., 163). Then, to make it clear the Shankill mural stories are additionally about class abuse, not sectarian division, the target is trained on Big House Unionism for it was they, rather than the Republicans, who were responsible for "poverty and squalor" in the interwar period. As we argue presently, this is needless to say, but the case that is being made is the case for a united working class within Northern Ireland within the UK.

Supposedly this more serious engagement allows an emphasis on the essentially working-class nature of Loyalism with its particular ideological and political variations. Various characters telling it like it is suggests a better way to understand Loyalism – it also therefore ensures a more sympathetic, in the sense of non-judgemental, reading of "who are the people" (Shirlow 2012, 15).

In arguing that Loyalists are not all "bad", not all street-fighting sectarian bigots, Shirlow draws an intriguing distinction between "mad dog" Loyalists – the "wreckers and spoilers" (108-132), characters such as Billy Wright ("King Rat") of the LVF (a breakaway from the UVF); Johnny Adair (UFF/UDA), leader of the notorious C Company of the UDA; and the others, the so-called "transitional"/"transformative" Loyalists (11-18). Leading examples of the latter in this scheme of things are Gusty

Spence (UVF), Billy Hutchinson (PUP, political wing of the UVF), David Ervine (UVF/PUP), and Dawn Purvis (PUP), who it is argued committed to a form of peaceful coexistence with Republicanism (essentially by this is meant living with the fact that Sinn Féin can play a role as partner in government – signing up to the 1998 GFA). This binary distinction is important and it allows for relatively straightforward opprobrium to be heaped upon the "wreckers" who can be dumped, in one instance as "regressive elements" (14) or in others as "unsavoury" and "irredentist elements" (200). Unlike these retro bigots, pining for a reinvented past of Orange supremacy, whingeing that the taigs got everything and "we, the People" got nothing, the "transformative" Loyalists have committed to leaving behind what amounts to a form of racism (102). Shirlow takes as an exemplar of "progressive" Loyalism the PUP's (UVF) *Principles of Loyalism* from 2002, which he interprets as,

> a comprehensive and deeply insightful account of the loyalist tradition and its location within the wider Unionist community. Noteworthy is the understanding of the meaning of the Union based upon citizenship and the removal of ethnic chauvinism and exclusivity. (102)

This document is indeed important. The *Principles* aim to commit Loyalism to a wider, secular view of Unionism and should be understood first and foremost as paean to a non-sectarian democracy:

> Citizenship for the British subject is not about national identity of cultural exclusiveness. It is about sharing a political identity that transcends religion, culture, language and ethnicity [...] it is about living in a multi-cultural and multi-ethnic pluralist society [...]. (cited in Shirlow 2012, 102)

This eulogy to the PUP is interesting. The temptation for us to wrap up the case against the idea that Loyalism can be a new secular vision is strong. We could end here letting this quotation itself stand as our criticism against the possibility that Loyalism can offer hope for a non-sectarian democracy. Because although it is clear from the excellent research data including the many interviews reported on that there are indeed significant differences between the so-called "wreckers" and those who penned the *Principles*, the "progressives", what unites them is what isn't made transparent, the great elephant in the room. The elephant is the character who is sitting apparently unseen: the "big grey one" limits in profoundly disturbing ways the extent of progressiveness that any kind of Loyalism can imagine let alone prosecute. We are given many instances of Loyalist opposition to the presumed Unionist bourgeoisie, of the refusal of many "progressives" to kowtow to Unionism and take up the (only rhetorical unfortunately) cudgels against poverty and social exclusion in Protestant working-class areas (ibid., 86) rejecting the DUP's sectarian dog-whistle blaming of all Protestant communities' social and economic woes on the IRA.

This is good and all very important. Yet one of the many reasons we find problems with the *Principles* is that like British nationalism more broadly, it fails to recognise the nationalism at the heart of its project for hegemonic control. If it doesn't seem like nationalism that is only because it doesn't need to. Like all imperial nationalisms its very security in its self-denying omnipotence means that it can often eschew the drumbeat of war. A good example of this was seen during the Scottish referendum in 2014 when British Unionists working under the auspices of Better Together, principally the Conservative and Labour parties, heaped opprobrium on the YES campaign for Scottish independence, describing it as solely a Nationalist movement and thus by implication against social inclusiveness. While they succeeded in undermining the vote for independence – though only just! – for this and other reasons, eventually the nature of the British establishment, which the left and the YES campaign had criticised from the start, was exposed as the most significant nationalism in the referendum, ultimately being described fairly for what it was – a BritNats front. The nationalism of the imperium does not need to be on display because "its" nationalism has won, or is winning. Songs and dances are only rarely called for. As Ian Jack, writing in the *Guardian* newspaper about the differences between the nationalism of a subordinate nation (he is discussing the phenomenon of Scottish nationalism) and the nationalism of the imperium put it, "the British nationalism of the rest of us was a norm that went largely [...] unremarked" (24 September 2016). Gordon MacIntyre-Kemp of the *National* was even more forceful in arguing that "conservative Unionism is unreconstructed British nationalism" (2 September 2016). The point here it that having won so many wars for so long, imperial powers, and in this case Britain, don't really need to hoist the flag terribly often, and when they do the pretence is that it's merely symbolic. As Greg McLaughlin and Stephen Baker, citing Michael Billig, put it, long-standing nation states "are inclined to see nationalism as the property and problem of others" (2015, 18).

Thus for "progressive" Loyalists to properly (that is, politically) challenge the UK state, the state which as they point out is leading to the further impoverishment of its (Protestant) own, they need to consider the extent to which this is possible while continuing to believe in the omnipotence of the "subject". Yet believing it is possible to challenge the state in *Protestant working-class* terms while fighting – preferably not on the street – to remain a "subject" allows the "good" Loyalists to continue in the daydream that it is not Britain as such that is undermining the British/Protestant working class but rather the current political elite. The clue then is also in the label "Protestant working class", which allows for the continuing myth that Protestant working-class relative economic disadvantage has in some sense been paid for by *Catholic working-class* relative advantage.

There is an arguably more disquieting feature of the narrative that suggests that one section of the working class is disadvantaged relative to another. The disquiet isn't to be found in recognising that, in the case of Northern Ireland, working-class Protestants do less well on a range of indices than working-class Catholics. As with all curate's eggs, the truth is exposed in the various ways in which it is displayed. Simply describing statistics of disadvantage across the UK and then citing figures for Protestant working-class failure while pointing out that Catholic working-class children do relatively better (one instance highlighted educational achievement) suggests that Catholic working-class children, and Catholics broadly speaking, are doing reasonably okay as a result of the GFA. That the GFA has now largely resolved the issue of Catholic exclusion and that all their Jacks are alright these days is very far from true as we know.

Furthermore, the fact that there are differences in, for example, educational attainment between working-class communities, is a problem for the working class together. It hasn't occurred perhaps that arguing about underachievement and other, economic, forms of poverty as if they can be seen as Protestant (or Catholic) specific leads to one and one conclusion only: only the Protestant working class can solve the problems facing the Protestant working class. We do not think this perspective leads us closer to the resolution of the complex issues surrounding working-class exclusion. It actually reinforces the legitimacy of those who seek resolution through the *Principles of Loyalism*: the good Loyalists. Perhaps this is the intention; if it is it will fail since, like the sectarian state that sustains it, it depends on working-class division. It is a form of pessimism to which we will return in our conclusion to the book.

Thus it really is the high commitment to the principle of the "Subject" in the first sentence of the *Principles* that makes our big elephant so visible. It is precisely this continued belief in the ultimate subservience to the Crown – the Crown as such, a Crown of subject(ion) – that is the problem. And it is this Crown of subjection that also by another twist of fate gives renewed vigour to this, the Unionist part, of the sectarian divide. We have seen how this works for both Catholic (Nationalist) and Protestant (Unionist) political classes in terms of political and economic patronage. However, what we can see is that while the accounts of differences of inflection, sometimes of substance, between the various Loyalist formations is vital in understanding the drivers and motivations with Loyalist traditions, what ultimately gives shape to Loyalism's trajectory is the changing character of the state in Northern Ireland.

Thus for Shirlow, since the soul of Loyalism, an ideology which in its best moments is neither sectarian nor inherently violent, is being fought over by "progressive" and "regressive" forces (23; 112), it should be obvious to any fair-minded observer which one must triumph. Otherwise the street fighters, the bigots will win. "Regressives" see the "progressives" as losers too, or people who are willingly capitulating to the enemy Catholic Nationalist hordes. In fact they are traitors to Loyalism and can be lumped in with the Shinners and the rest since they are seen by "regressive" Loyalists as "'capitulators' who were signing up to a pan-Nationalist constructed and driven peace process" (ibid.,113; 110).

Thus, if the purpose is to show that while "King Rat" and his wreckers are authentic, and his supporters have understandable if often abhorrent ideas with equally vile ways of achieving them, there exists another, gentler, emollient kind of Loyalism. Because the "progressives" are committed to compromise, their aims and objectives are thus poles apart from the "ethno-sectarian" militarist wreckers, despite having the same adherence to the UK state and Protestantism. It's about choosing between guns and flags on the one side or neatly manicured parliamentary procedure on the other. If working-class Protestantism, Loyalism, ditches the rabble, though authentic enough, then it can move forward:

> Loyalists must emerge out of a wider sloth-like body that has impeded their potential. It is not an end to Ulster Loyalism that is required, but the cessation of de-stabilising elements and actions from within. To be a volunteer or defender should never be a rhetorical guise but an earned title tied to inclusive actions that aim for justice, inclusion and social emancipation. Loyalism cannot, as a discourse, organisation or set of ideas remain as a one-size-fits-all body when some participants do not embrace or abide by socially transformative principles. (Ibid., 206)

Nonetheless, interesting though this injunction is, moralism included, from our standpoint the difference between variants of Loyalism and Unionism cannot be explained unless understood in relation to the state. This does not mean that we reduce Loyalism, especially Shirlow's "bad" Loyalism, to a motive of state strategy or merely to a space where bigots and Orange fools can play their Lambeg drums. There is sufficient evidence including our brief references here to the sometimes easy slippage between the activities of Big and Small House Unionists to tell us that the goodies and baddies have always coexisted, from those chasing "rotten prods" from the shipyards to those marching on tiny hamlets in the Irish republic, to those waving union flags outside Belfast city hall, never mind the violence of the UDA's C Company....

What therefore principally distinguishes Protestant Unionism from Protestant Loyalism (the proposed "good" and "bad" variants) is not class or attitudes to extra-parliamentary action. Class matters, and clearly the difference in the social composition of Ulster Unionism and Ulster Loyalism is evident enough – no more obviously so where the latter, as has been recognised, addresses issues of social and economic depredation. But the political characteristics of these political forms and their respective ideologies coalesce around the central commitment to the hegemony of the British state, the British queen and subordination not simply of *Irish* republicanism but of republicanism as such. At different times in the history of the state in Northern Ireland Protestant culture and political society (if these even exist in hermetic spaces beyond Irishness: in case of doubt see the late great John Hewitt's life work) as we have illustrated, the state's repressive forces and institutions before and after 1972 contained, while they constrained, extra-parliamentary Unionism-Loyalism.

Which begs the question, how can we better understand the character of so-called Loyalism? This is important because if the objectives of all the goodies have been, or should be, to encourage those committed to "socially transformative principles" (Shirlow 2012, 206) then we need to know why the baddies, those "de-stabilising elements and actions from within", continue to reappear, to reproduce time and again. Possibly the acutest recent understanding to the activities of working-class Protestants described as loyalists has come from Bea Campbell (2008). We agree with her perspective that sets out to interpret the actions of Loyalist organisations, and individuals, since 1998, in the context of the practices and institutions of the Northern Ireland state: the new sectarian state.

Since our argument is that we can only understand the state by looking at it in relation to what has gone before, we also need to explore the ways in which relationships with the British state have evolved since 1998. Quite simply, the GFA, whatever the critical role played by Republicans, Irish

Nationalists, Loyalists and Unionists in publicly declaring an end to the older sectarian state, was contrived to maintain British hegemony not just with regards to the final text of the Agreement. This hegemony amounted to much more than a textual, or discursive, control of language. It was more than wordplay. It was based upon real, material control of a key aspect of state strategy that was seen as crucial for both the retrenchment *and reinvention* of UK state control of the north.

Ensuring British hegemony depended upon the maintenance of two mutually sustaining sets of relationships. The first was between the respective "victors" as the media described them, often derisorily, and the British state. Often the "victors" would change according to the needs of the media and the state so that at one moment it could be that old saw, "the men of violence",[7] and at others it might be the Protestants, so as to make the Prods feel they hadn't lost out. For the BBC journalist Peter Taylor, his perplexity at Protestant grievance is heightened by his belief that the Prods won (see *Irish News*, 26 September 2014: "British and Unionists Won 'War' Says Troubles Journalist Peter Taylor"). Perhaps he meant that the British won the war? For us, both the Prods and the Taigs have lost out, though the extent of loss depends, inevitably, upon one's class position. Keynesianism and increased public spending were important to keep both "Orange" and "Green" relatively quiescent. The second set of relationships that required maintenance, arguably more controversially, was between the new state and the former sectarian Orange state. This is less well understood.

This distinction is important because often the GFA has been interpreted as signalling a profound shift in political institutions, civic representation and state-civil society

7   Since the spoils of the war (the Assembly largesse) began to trickle all the way from the top of the top to the bottom of the top, the whingers within the Stormont political class have become less audible.

relationships. The emphasis in mainstream commentary has been placed on the goodly sounding parts of the Agreement committing to a new-found realm of civic and political tolerance. We would not entirely disagree for example, with Bea Campbell's view that the GFA was a "thing of beauty" (2008). This sentiment is reasonable insofar as the written promises contained within, and the public expectations surrounding it, spoke to a different history, a new landscape free of sectarian values and bounded by a secular commitment to democratic, egalitarian civil and political aspirations. However, it is precisely the GFA's real-world limitations that she finds noteworthy.

The fact that it has not worked out as anticipated requires explanation, some of which has been covered elsewhere. Bea Campbell eloquently identifies the difference between intent and outcome of the GFA, even going so far as accounting for the origins of its dark side, the new repressive state. Arguably she may, however, despite her exploration of its repressive origins in the fight between the modernisers and the deep British state (not her terms), have actually underestimated the degree to which the retrenchment of sectarianism is not just contradictory in the long term. Being contradictory is evident enough: there is a paradox between the optimism of the Agreement and the grubby reality of enduring sectarian conflict. Our argument is that the sectarianism of everyday life and the many fine, lyrical hymns to cross-community endearment are perfectly complementary. The contradiction, in other words, is only apparent. It is the new sectarian state that sustains this "contradiction", depending upon it to a great extent: Shirlow's street-fighting Loyalists and the Stormont-headed notepaper Loyalists, including the Big House Unionists when circumstances demand, jostle for position according to the situation. The way they play to Irish nationalism, to those living in predominantly Catholic communities but as much to those living in their own, is a product of the new sectarian state and in some respects, as an illustration of its apparent paralysis, the very definition of it. Except that it only seems to be transfixed, paralysed, by the spectre of Loyalism on the streets if we assume that it finds street-fighting Loyalists an existential problem for the Northern Ireland Assembly and the GFA. As Bea Campbell has reminded us, it's supposed to be like this. Illustrating her argument by reference to young children being intimidated on their way to Holy Cross school in north Belfast in 2001, she writes,

> Nothing like it had ever happened before. The route to school of little catholic girls was blockaded by unionist men, often hiding their faces behind Rangers Football Club scarves or baseball caps [...] Between the blockade and the girls stood a barricade of riot police in their Darth Vader livery, but the RUIC was inexplicably facing the girls rather than their unionist assailants, who were throwing improvised missiles over the heads of the unseeing police: paint balloons, dog shit, hot tea, urine, and even a pipe bomb. (145)

But what this singular (daily) assault illustrated in despicable and stark fashion was the practical, everyday workings of the new sectarian state:

> Behind the blockade were institutions that behaved with decorous inertia. Apart from the daily mass mobilisation of the police, the scaffolding of Northern Ireland's institutions remained unshaken by the atrocity of Holy Cross. That inertia was not nothing, however: it was an achievement. It required thought and effort to do nothing to stop the picketing of the children. The institutions, in effect, decided to be untouched by the Agreement during the opportunity offered by Holy Cross. (Ibid., 146)

For Campbell, "The, institutions, in effect, decided to be untouched by the Agreement," because this is exactly what is permitted by it, and it is in the detail of permissiveness that the new sectarianism creeps out. What the Holy Cross assault illustrates is the reproduction of the Unionist side of the new sectarian divide: it's the reproduction of what we term Unionist-Loyalist politics. Thus, we see no contradiction between the great Agreement on paper and sectarian division in everyday life. They only appear contradictory when the view is from the written end of the Agreement's telescope, the end that casts everything as renewal, as clean and revived, as a break with the past. When seen from the other, entrenched, old society end, the telescope is able to pick out continuity, revival for sure, but a revival that also allows for older antipathies to thrive.

What we are describing is the importance of the old sectarianism in the body politic of the new sectarian state. Societies do not appear ready-made, cast down from blue skies, since they are also cast up from the dark, peaty earth of their past. Sad to say, but the Agreement was made from the substance of the north's sectarian realities, not from the ideals of its paper virtues (Campbell 2008). Of course those paper virtues – cross-sectarian communitarianism, fairness at work, a Civic Forum – matter(ed),[8] but the background

8   The following is quoted from the executive summary of Ray McCaffrey's 5 September 2013 research paper titled *The Civic Forum*:

The Civic Forum emerged from the Belfast (Good Friday) Agreement as part of the institutions established under Strand One of the Agreement. The Forum comprised 60 representatives from the business, trade union, voluntary sectors etc. and was to act as a consultative mechanism on social, economic and cultural issues. The Forum met in Plenary 12 times between October 2000 and October 2002, when the political institutions were suspended. The advent of the Forum was not universally welcomed by elected representatives. There was a view among some Members of the Assembly that its membership did not adequately represent the views

noise was of a fight over the spoils of compromise. This is not a discussion about how to increase the spoils for all our people, whether of Protestant, Catholic or any other (or simply no) persuasion.

Sectarian Protestant political parties, while reflecting the interests of people in specific communities, do so in particular ways in certain circumstances. While it is nonsense to define the Protestant working class as reactionary, such a view has long been the bugbear of radical political analysis. Shirlow has highlighted often forgotten and important aspects of this politics, not the least the fight against poverty, against inadequate housing and for progress in community development programmes. He makes the point that in a Northern Ireland where nearly a quarter of children live in poverty, and where they "are twice as likely to be living in persistent poverty compared with those living in Britain" (203) it is only the "transitional and progressive Loyalists" (203) from within Unionism, as he describes it, who challenge this in Protestant communities. Yet the problem is that the agenda he sets out for them (204) cannot be met this side of a wider social transformation and specifically the end of the new sectarian state which requires too a

of those in society who had voted against the Agreement and that it was an unnecessary additional layer of bureaucracy, whose funding could be better used elsewhere. Supporters of the Forum argued that it was a valuable mechanism for obtaining the views of wider civic society and bridging the gap between political institutions and the public. During its operation, the Forum produced a number of reports on issues such as Human Rights, Lifelong Learning, and Sustainable Development along with submissions on the Programme for Government. There were differing opinions among members of the Forum as to the effectiveness of the Forum, with some positive about the ability of the Forum to influence change, while others questioned the willingness of the Assembly and Executive to take account of its views.

rejection of neo-liberalism. The argument that working-class Loyalists – where they shed forever their street-fighting ways and forever renounce the "corrosiveness of remaining criminality" (203) – can sustain a cross-sectarian working-class agenda while remaining Loyal to state is premised precisely on working-class division: within the UK. It may anyway be improbable anytime soon, but for sure, with state institutions and a repressive apparatus standing by while practically sustaining sectarianism, as we saw with Holy Cross, Loyalists of any hue, whatever the size of their house, will not be able to challenge the social and economic exclusions Shirlow so carefully elaborates. The clue is in the descriptor – Loyalism.

Work in the 1970s by Geoffrey Bell (1976) and others, notably Michael Farrell (1976), though very important in telling a story that was really quite unknown in Britain, and even in parts of Northern Ireland beyond Catholic communities, about the deeply dysfunctional Orange state, had a tendency to draw an equal sign between Protestant working-class communities and the parties they supported. Let us not forget that this work, though ground-breaking, overly simplified the relation between people, their communities and their political affiliations and parties. That said, the story these writers gave us required telling in plain terms at the time. These parties were – with the persistence of the DUP and others – sectarian and, especially with the DUP, proudly so. Protestants continue to vote for them in their tens of thousands, but understanding this cannot be explained by looking at divided communities on their own.

In conclusion, our argument has been that the best way of making sense of the various characters, actions and divisions within Unionist-Loyalist politics is by placing them in a political context. As has been demonstrated previously in writing about political forces and state strategy in Northern Ireland (prominently by Bell 1976; Farrell 1976; O'Dowd et al. 1980; McKearney 2011), context is everything. Thus, we argued that the recent highly vocal expression of Unionist politics in the form of Loyalism only began to emerge in a distinctive way beginning in the early 1970s. The Orange state began its long terminal decline and the space for a Protestant-Unionist militia (the B-Specials) was reined in by Britain to be replaced by the UDR which played a similar though redefined role. While the B-Specials were concerned to police and control the Catholic community between 1920 and 1972, searching for signs of disaffection, the UDR functioned to subordinate the Catholic community and notably those insurgents who emerged from within it beginning in 1969.

This is not what Loyalism is however. On the contrary, Loyalism is not another term for a Protestant militia. This is not our argument – Loyalism cannot be explained by dividing it between the bad guys (the guns) and the good guys (Stormont-headed notepaper) because "Unionists" too liked the gun, as we saw. If anything, Loyalism represents the great shape-shifter of Irish Protestant working-class politics, the politics of community domination: first of various Catholic communities, then of its own, Protestant working-class communities. In short, Loyalism is concerned with finding ways of mobilising Protestants from within predominantly – but not exclusively – working-class communities in order to defend the relationship between Britain and the northern part of Ireland from a number of points of political and social departure. It is not inherently concerned with street protest, but when Unionists take to the streets, usually, but not only as we have seen, led by those from working-class communities, it is easy to use the appellation of Loyalist. For sure, there are differences, mostly of class, between so-called Unionists and so-called Loyalists which it is ridiculous to deny: the sociology of participants in the UUP, the DUP and the UVF's PUP speaks for itself. But while the differences between the various class and social narratives within Big House Unionism and Small House

Loyalism matter, allowing, as Shirlow points out, the kind of demands made by the PUP, for example, that the UUP and DUP would simply never countenance, the reasons the so-called "progressive Loyalists" can never achieve their demands are fundamentally due to their committed subservience to Britain. This is ultimately a dependence on political and economic subordination. After Partition, Loyalist expressions of street and flag-waving dissent were largely absent due to the strength of the Orange state. Since 1998, the space for Protestants who have not benefited very much from the GFA has been limited. From being active participants in the Orange state, including its Protestant sectarian largesse supporting industrial employment and regional development assistance, Protestants are now having to share the crumbs from the table of the new cross-sectarian political (and economic) class which places them more or less in the same forgotten space as those in Falls and the Bogside.

Chapter 4

Northern Ireland: The Failed State

Alone among Northern Ireland's Unionist leaders, First Minister Peter Robinson had appeared willing, on occasions, to accept reality and recognise the developing and changing nature of the area's political make-up. Speaking at his party's spring conference in Newcastle Co. Down on 12 April 2014, Mr Robinson told DUP colleagues that demographic changes could not be wished away and ignoring them would be what he termed, "constitutionally dangerous". The North's First Minister said the test of success for Unionist parties would be to stop looking for Lundies and look instead for converts. Significantly, this part of his speech went almost unreported in the local press, and no other Unionist politician seemed prepared or able to share his well-founded concerns about the six-county state's future.

No matter how crude and vulgar the sectarian headcount may be in terms of democratic politics, it has long informed much of political life in the North of Ireland. From the founding of the six-county state, Unionism sought to control the numbers. Since the demise of the old Orange state this is no longer possible and an underlining current reality is the most recent 2011 census, which indicated a declining Unionist majority.

Between the 2001 census and the 2011 census, the Protestant community in Northern Ireland declined from 53% to 48% of the population while the Roman Catholic percentage increased from 44% to 45%. There were a significant percentage of people (5.6%) defining themselves as of no religion but this does not alter the underlying trend, especially when the age profile in each

And the posters
say it all – except
that it isn't all that's
really meant.

DON'T KNOW WHO SHOULD BE IN INTENSIVE CARE; US OR THE POOR OLD N.H.S.

False shop and house fronts in Dungannon attempt to mask economic and urban decline. (Photos by Gearóid Ó Machail)

Photo by kind permission of Radek Polkowski.

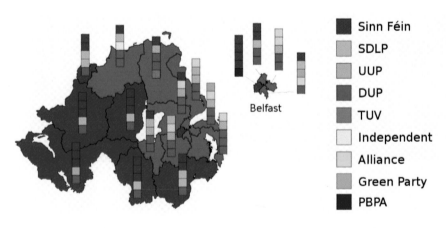

Belfast

- Sinn Féin
- SDLP
- UUP
- DUP
- TUV
- Independent
- Alliance
- Green Party
- PBPA

Electoral map of Northern Ireland after the March 2017 Assembly Election (DrKay and Furfur 2017, via Wikipedia). Note the contraction of unionism.

group is considered. In Northern Ireland, among the oldest age groups, Protestants and "Other Christians" outnumber Catholics by around two to one, whereas Catholics outnumber Protestants and "Other Christians" within each age group under forty.

There is awareness among Unionist politicians and their supporters of this inexorable trend and it has led to Unionism resorting to practices that in the past resulted in high levels of discontent. A report in the Web-based journal *The Detail* in June 2012 pointed to the DUP's Minister for Social Development in the Northern Ireland Executive, Nelson McCausland, giving special housing preference for loyalist areas. This was one of the main grievances of the Civil Rights movement in the late 1960s and in the opinion of many was a major factor for the violence that followed. Since then we have witnessed the emergence of race-based housing disputes. There has been the unedifying sight of Northern Ireland's First Minister Peter Robinson attempting to claim that efforts to prevent a Nigerian family being housed in a Unionist district were not racist in origin and this in spite of his recognition of the changing nature of the region's demographics.

Unionism is currently taking comfort from a shaky assumption that in the event of there no longer being a Protestant majority in Northern Ireland, a significant percentage of middle-class Catholics will vote for their wallets and opt to remain in the UK. This is by no means a certainty since the Republic of Ireland's upper middle class and professional class have remained remarkably well off and content in spite of the recession. Political unification would not necessarily, therefore, have a noticeable economic impact on that cohort of the population expected to change allegiance and vote Unionist.

Other factors are combining to make the Unionist position ever more precarious. The referendum campaign in Scotland, for example, raised blunt questions about the permanency of the United Kingdom as currently constituted. While in 2014 Scotland voted to remain in the UK, many commentators of both Scottish and British nationalism recognise the future for an integral UK remains bleak due to the fact that the question of Scottish independence continues like an open wound, raising disturbing questions for all Unionists in Northern Ireland.

Most significant of all the factors external to Northern Ireland control is that the economic rationale underpinning the union has been steadily eroded over the past few decades, paradoxically due largely to the efforts of Margaret Thatcher and her supporters. As Britain's ruling class sought to reinforce its position by redirecting the state's economy away from manual-labour-dependent coal and steel and towards London-centric financial services, peripheral regions have grown less crucial to the needs of the governing elite.

Writing about London in a 2014 *Financial Times* article, Gillian Tett said,

> when some economists from Deutsche Bank recently looked at the city, they discovered … London is driven by global trading flows, not the British economy. "The overall pattern that emerges […] is one of the rest of the UK dancing to the capital's tune but out of time," they wrote.

In terms of the overall British economy, Northern Ireland is now the least crucial region of all and well out of kilter with the rest of the United Kingdom.

Set against this inauspicious backdrop for Northern Ireland Unionism is a slew of dismal statistics and reports illustrating the region as a failing social and economic entity. A 2014 *Belfast Telegraph* survey claimed that two-thirds of sixteen- to twenty-four-year-olds in the North believe that they shall emigrate (Clarke 2014).

The Centre for Economics and Business Research's monthly "income tracker" found that discretionary incomes in Northern Ireland are less than half of the wider UK average. Research findings released by the New Policy Institute for the Joseph Rowntree Foundation reported that Northern Ireland's labour market and poverty rates have deteriorated in the last five years, and welfare reforms are likely to exacerbate these problems.

Northern Ireland ranks bottom of almost all measures of economic prosperity (or poverty) in the United Kingdom. For example, the Annual Survey of Hours and Earnings (ASHE) in the six counties for 2013 demonstrated that yearly growth in median gross weekly earnings for all employees (i.e. both full- and part-time) in the area was 1.7% (to £367), compared to the UK where earnings increased by 2.6% (to £417). NI full-time employees' gross weekly earnings at April 2013 were £460, which was 88.9% of the figure in the UK (£518). NI full-time earnings increased by 0.5% over the period, compared with an increase of 2.2% in the UK. Full-time weekly private sector earnings in NI increased over the year by 2.3% (to £403). This represented no change to the NI/UK private sector pay gap, which remains at 82.1% of the UK figure. Part-time private sector earnings grew 7.9% (to £132).

Not that the impact of these statistics are confined to the dry reports of officialdom. The *Belfast Telegraph* of 16 June 2014 reported almost exactly the same under the following headline: "Northern Irish Workers: Huge Wage Divide Compared to UK Peers Doing Same Job: Figures Reveal Huge Wage Divide in Labour Market". Declining wages and the consequent increase in poverty can be seen in the rise of food banks in the north. According to the Trussell Trust (see introduction) there was a forty-eight per cent increase in their use during the year up to April 2016: "In 2015-16 emergency three-day food packages were needed in Northern Ireland 25,755 times, compared to last year's figure of 17,425" (*Belfast Telegraph*, 15 April 2016).

Exacerbating this poor economic state of affairs is the fact that the Northern Ireland Assembly has no realistic and proactive plan to alter the situation. In her first annual monitoring report on the Northern Ireland economic strategy, Arlene Foster, then Minister of Enterprise, Trade and Investment, resorted to the usual old shibboleths such as weakness in global economic conditions and the need to reduce the rate of corporation tax to the same level as that in the Republic. Factors such as the international economic crisis and rates of tax undoubtedly have an impact on an economy but they do so vicariously or indirectly. The Northern Ireland economy requires positive intervention, and the free-market, neo-liberal consensus prevailing in London and blindly adhered to in Belfast prevents this type of necessary intervention.

Compounding this dismal snapshot of social and economic life is a stagnant political environment so unproductive that many no longer even wish to cast a ballot. Alex Kane, a former adviser to David Trimble, recently wrote in the *News Letter* that he would not vote in the local government elections because, as he says, "the Assembly isn't working, the Executive is dysfunctional, we have farce rather than government, the parties don't care; and nothing is being allowed to change" (21 April 2014).

Kane was not just highlighting the stalemate in the Northern Assembly but also echoed in his article the words of Theresa Villiers, the British Conservative Secretary of State for the North, who had bluntly warned local Northern Irish politicians that if Stormont cannot evolve it may well collapse. She pointedly reminded them in her speech that a state that doesn't have the means to change is also a state without the means of its own preservation.

Ms Villiers' words carry a more profound meaning than many of her audience realised because they surely reveal a long-term change in Britain's Irish policy. This is a change not relating to the North alone but one pointing towards a recalibration of London's policy towards all of Ireland. Over the past few decades, Britain has invested considerable political and military capital in the "Ulster Question". Now, while Whitehall is undoubtedly content it no longer has to contend with frequent bombings and gun battles, there is clearly still a sense of frustration with the never-ending political deadlock in Belfast. Moreover, this exasperation has no doubt caused London to view Northern Ireland as unstable or even unmanageable and therefore not the best possible fit for its wider requirements.

There is, moreover, the more mundane calculation that it is in the British ruling class's best interests to ensure that the only other English-speaking member of the EU is encouraged to subscribe to a broadly similar economic and global consensus as that promoted by Westminster. London might be unfazed by the Republic participating in the Euro monetary zone, but would be deeply concerned if Dublin were to sign exclusive trade agreements with Russia and China, for example.

At the beginning of the twentieth century, more enlightened members of Britain's ruling class believed that interests such as these were best secured through an Irish home-rule parliament. When this arrangement failed, the Northern state offered a similar foothold, albeit one less satisfactory than having the complicity of the whole island. Events are now apparently turning back in favour of the older concept of a southern Irish parliament willingly embracing a closer relationship with Britain. Some are even mentioning having the twenty-six counties back in the Commonwealth. From a British government perspective, this is an agreeable and viable option and one worth promoting through the diplomatic offensive now under way with state visits to Windsor Castle and concerts in the Royal Albert Hall.

Where, therefore, does Northern Ireland rank in this scenario, in light of what Lord Palmerston once defined as Britain's "eternal and perpetual interests"? The answer is, not very highly as London will gladly swap Belfast for Dublin. Peter Robinson is probably as aware of this as he is alert to changing demographics. The question is whether the rest of Northern Ireland can find a positive solution to this changing reality.

Several decades back, a former Taoiseach, Charles Haughey, described Northern Ireland as a failed political entity. There is little evidence at present to suggest that his assessment has been proven incorrect. Unionist leaders may be aware of just how precarious is their hold on office and influence but can do little to alter their situation as Unionism appears incapable of acting in its own best interests.

For Northern Ireland to retain its current status quo and remain part of the United Kingdom, there needs to be a consensus on its present and future. This would demand a very energetic "hearts and minds" offensive directed at the North's Catholic community coupled with an agreement to accept responsibility for a portion of the failings of the past. No Unionist politician could possibly hope to be elected on such a platform and by extension this means that Northern Ireland remains and will continue to remain a failed state with only one reasonable option – to build anew on a very different social and economic foundation. Yet, how realistic is this at present? How bad can it be for us to think the whole stable needs rebuilding? Lest readers think us churlish, let us take a brief look into the purer, nobler soul of the economics behind the politics for while the people in the north, Protestant and Catholic (and the rest) alike, can agree at least on something, there is some hope that change will come to the politics of the Assembly and its gathered mini multitude. How bad is it?

From Orange patronage to rainbow patronage: "Discrimination for all"; "One person one moat"; "Housing for everyone, especially our own"

We made these banner headlines up since, it goes without saying, no political party would put these on its banner, but in the way of many Orwellian precepts, characteristic of the dystopia of society in the north, it is hard to take notions of democratic progress at face value. Stating that everyone at Stormont is against sectarianism, as if sectarianism was simply a description of a deranged cast of mind that likes to "think" before shouting nasty things at people as a result of their religious preference, is giving too much credence to the power of thought over the realities it creates. The north is a sectarian society not only because people say and assume nasty things about "the other" due to the nature of their reading of the Christian bible. It is sectarian, first because it always has been – that was its original purpose in 1998 – and second because the institutions which define that state (in housing, health and welfare, and economic strategies) depend upon reinforcing sectarian distribution of economic power, including economic resources, to the two predetermined sides of the divide between Protestant and Catholic communities. The purpose of the state here, the Northern Ireland Assembly, is to ensure that sectarian divisions are not only manifest in deranged minds but in fact are sustained by a mutually reinforcing political consensus upon which rests the north's political elite.

Of course, no political entity anywhere has a monopoly over the use of discriminatory patronage or pork-barrel politics. In Northern Ireland however, unfair use of patronage originally manifested itself through a sectarian filter affording privilege to the pro-union population.

This practice became so widespread that for a time it was almost taken for granted. Systemic discriminatory practice, delivered via the state, was the material basis from which arose decades of civil unrest. Misgovernment was midwife to the armed insurrection, which characterised life in the northern part of Ireland throughout the last quarter of the twentieth century.

The Republican insurrection of the late twentieth century failed in its primary stated objective of breaking the political connection between the six-county political entity and Britain. It did, however, bring an end to the old Orange state with its explicit ethos of a "Protestant parliament for a Protestant people",[9] as even Peter Taylor, no friend of the Republican movement by any stretch of the imagination, pointed out when highlighting the importance of the insurgency in "breaking the mould of the Unionist state" (*Irish News*, 26 September 2014). The British government realised early in the 1970s that it was not tenable in the long run to have Northern Ireland governed undemocratically by one section of the community.

London eventually managed, through the GFA, to create a cross-party administration that at least addressed the one-sided nature of the original arrangement. This led to the emergence of a new and different set of power relationships, which certainly swept aside the old Orange state but replaced it with a new equally sectarian arrangement or, as has been said, an Orange and Green state. Although less obviously undemocratic than the *ancien régime*, it has ominous echoes of the separate but equal ethos of apartheid. We use the term advisedly. There are no racial card checks and no large urban sites of subhuman habitation though there are significant sites of poverty and deprivation: everyone

9   See the article "A Protestant Parliament for a Protestant People" at http://www.historyireland.com/20th-century-contemporary-history/a-protestant-parliament-for-a-protestant-people-2/

now has an indoor toilet and we all have running water. The accommodation of sectarianism – not overcoming it. More than this, and as we have argued, persistent, blatant sectarianism is being recodified in Northern Ireland, and nowhere is the retrenchment of tribal identity more starkly evidenced in the realm of social policy than within the education sector.

Despite persistent international pressure on the DUP/SF coalition to ameliorate the religious apartheid model of education in the Northern Ireland state, the integrated education sector consistently complains about an ongoing lack of proactive support. Instead, the Stormont authorities have sought to appease the US and British sponsors of the "peace process" by proposing modification of existing structures of educational provision currently on offer from both the northern state and its proxy, the Roman Catholic Church.

As part of the Stormont House Agreement, configured to resolve yet another Stormont crisis, the British government said it would provide support of up to £500 million over ten years of new capital funding to support shared and integrated education projects. Plans were announced to build ten shared education campuses but little progress has been made since the campuses idea was first announced in 2013.

In 2015 the Education Minister launched a consultation on the Executive's proposals for "Shared Education". Both successive Sinn Féin and DUP education ministers have sought to reframe policy away from the concept of "integrated education" and towards the Stormont Executive's preferred policy of "shared education". The Executive has purposefully posited a straight fight for resources between the two forms of education.

Educational experts, including Sir Bob Salisbury, have labelled the exercise as "patently absurd", saying the only things some children will share are toilets and playgrounds

(*Irish News*, 19 November 2015). The policy has echoes of the nineteenth-century "separate but equal" legal doctrine in the United States. Under the doctrine, as long as the facilities provided to each race were equal, state and local governments could require that services, facilities, public accommodations, housing, medical care, education, employment, and transportation be segregated by race. The repeal of such restrictive laws, generally known as Jim Crow laws, was a key focus of the Civil Rights Movement in the US.

A total of sixteen projects involving more than fifty schools were competing for funding but former Education Minister John O'Dowd approved just three. A BBC *Spotlight* programme on one of the initial projects involving the two primary schools in The Moy, Co. Tyrone, showed clearly the difference between "Shared Education" and "Integrated Education".[10] "Shared" means pupils of different religions under one roof but with separate doors into separate facilities, with separate dinner times, separate uniforms, separate lessons etc.

Tellingly, "separate but equal" provision of children's education in twenty-first-century Northern Ireland is sold as a post-conflict panacea for sectarian division. Stormont Executive efforts to bring state-controlled schools and Roman Catholic-maintained schools on to shared geographical sites are trumpeted by party spokespersons as progressive social policy. Despite that, even limited cross-community engagement as exemplified by the flagship "shared educational campus" projects in the town of Omagh and in Armagh City have been extremely slow to come to fruition. In the latter case, opposition from the Roman Catholic Church authorities has effectively scuppered the "shared educational village" plans.

10   For more information, see https://www.bbc.co.uk/
     programmes/b04tr4qq; http://www.bbc.com/news/
     uk-northern-ireland-34270448; http://www.bbc.com/news/
     uk-northern-ireland-28105101

Nonetheless the policy of "separate but equal" remains the Stormont Executive's preferred policy, despite the rapidly changing demographic within Northern Ireland. While the general populace is becoming less reluctant in many areas to ascribe confessional identities to either themselves or to their children, the DUP/SF coalition appears determined to retain and support the sectarian status quo. This persistent focus on communal identity poses added difficulties for the growing population of families and children arriving in Northern Ireland from other countries in search of work and a new life.

In order to prevent a return to one-party rule by Unionism, the authors of the agreement inserted the complex D'Hondt set of procedures, ensuring that no legislation could pass without cross-party (cross-community) consent.[11] To gauge the existence (or lack thereof) of a sufficient level of agreement, elected representatives had first to designate themselves as either Unionist or Nationalist, which in effect perpetuated the existence of sectarianism.

An immediate difficulty for the GFA was that it was not what either of the two largest parties (the DUP and Sinn Féin) sought as their ideal solution. The hard-line DUP had pursued a reactionary and populist set of demands seeking the total military destruction of the republican insurrection and with it, a return to the status quo ante. This brought about a situation where to maintain support they had to appear more hostile to Sinn Féin than their Unionist rivals. Sinn Féin on the other hand had depended for so much support on the IRA organisation and support base that it too would have been in a delicate position if forced to admit that it had agreed to administer the state it had for so long pledged to smash.

Nevertheless this has not led to a collapse of the

---

11 For more details on the D'Hondt system for picking NI ministers in Stormont, see http://www.bbc.com/news/uk-northern-ireland-politics-13359731

devolved government in Northern Ireland. What it has caused, however, is ongoing stagnation and stoppage and a condition of almost permanent political paralysis. One aspect of representative, as distinct from participatory, democracy is that a shared interest in maintaining the apparatus of government can often allow apparently divergent or even antagonistic opinions to be accommodated. In a sense this appears to be what happened in November 2015 when Sinn Féin and the DUP agreed to what has been described as a humiliation for both. The drama that had begun in September 2015 with allegations that Sinn Féin was still controlled by the IRA appeared, on the surface, to have the potential to bring an end to devolved government. The dispute ended, however, after weeks of tedious negotiations, with a tame agreement to carry on much as before.

Of course, the real issue was not really about the IRA since both the DUP and the UUP were well aware of what that organisation was or was not doing. As First Minister of Northern Ireland, Peter Robinson had routine access to the chief constable's security assessments. Moreover, he could easily confirm any analysis received from the PSNI's Chief Constable George Hamilton through the many senior police officers who are also members of the DUP and Free Presbyterian Church. What caused the 2015 Stormont spat was, on one level, the result of a desperate attempt by the UUP leadership to recover ground lost to its DUP rival. However, the breakdown was symptomatic of a much deeper malaise and that is the very nature of the Northern Ireland state and its sclerotic political institutions.

Gone are the days when the North was of vital strategic interest to Britain's global ambitions. Gone too are the days when the area's heavy industries and agricultural produce were of economic significance to the British Exchequer and state. In fact, gone are the days when Northern Ireland or its political institutions could exert any significant influence over policymaking as it develops and is delivered from Westminster, the current relationship between the DUP and the Tories notwithstanding. The area is now in a political limbo. Its devolved administration has neither the clout to influence central government nor does it enjoy sufficient local consensus to do as the Scots, and work towards meaningful autonomy.

As a consequence, the Assembly was ultimately obliged to accept London's agenda for the region. In the first instance it had to oversee the administration of a right-wing Tory government agenda with its endless round of austerity measures. Sinn Féin was critical of the Welfare Reform Act but could only delay its implementation and then only at the risk of undermining the institutions. As for Unionists' demands that Sinn Féin be chastised for its connections to the IRA, the outcome was yet another unenforceable requirement that Stormont ministers promise not to encourage paramilitaries. Caught in this stagnant world, Stormont has lapsed into veniality, all too often serving the narrow sectional and sectarian interests of the North's political class.

People in the north of Ireland have very qualified respect for the devolved political institutions and the politicians tasked with the administration of the region. In light of many episodes of dubious practice, it is small surprise that they are viewed with such jaundiced eyes. In 2011 for example, DUP ministers lobbied the NIHE, a statutory agency, to retain the services of the Red Sky construction company after the firm had been found in breach of a series of regulations, including overcharging the public purse (*The Detail*, 12 September 2012). When DUP involvement in the case came to light, the party simply closed off the investigation by using its majority in the Assembly to lodge a petition of concern. Interestingly too, Frank Cushnahan, a former director of the Red Sky Company, was nominated by

DUP Minister Sammy Wilson to sit on NAMA's Northern committee.[12] While it has to be said that none of the above has resulted to date in legal action or sanction, there is undoubtedly more than a hint of sharp practice about it.

The nexus of political interests ranges widely across northern society and it remains difficult to prove wrongdoing. Nevertheless, the feeling that something is not quite what it seems remains ever-present. Take for example the spectacular rise of DUP Assembly member Emma Little-Pengelly. Mrs Little-Pengelly was appointed a junior minister in the Office of the First Minister and Deputy First Minister (OFMDFM) a mere four weeks after being co-opted as a MLA for South Belfast. Prior to her elevation to Assembly membership she had acted as a special adviser to the then First Minister Peter Robinson and before that to the late Ian Paisley.

While Mrs Little-Pengelly was enjoying her promotion, her husband Richard was under pressure at Stormont's finance committee, which was examining the £1.2 billion sale of NAMA's northern portfolio to US investment firm Cerberus (*Belfast Telegraph*, 11 November 2015). A senior official at the Department of Finance until December 2012, Mr Pengelly told MLAs he could not recall the specifics of meetings or discussions around the nomination of him and two others to the NAMA advisory board. In spite of her husband's stressful position, the new junior minister nevertheless appeared able to cope, due perhaps to her previous experience of having a parent imprisoned.

Her father, Noel Little, a civil servant and founder member in 1986 with Peter Robinson and Ian Paisley of Ulster Resistance, was arrested in connection with an

12   NAMA: The National Asset Management Agency is a body created by the government of Ireland in late 2009, in response to the Irish financial crisis and the deflation of the Irish property bubble. For more details see https://www.nama.ie/about-us/

alleged plot to smuggle weapons from Apartheid South Africa into Northern Ireland (*Irish Times*, 28 October 2015). Little was arrested in Paris in April 1989 in the company of a South African diplomat with parts of a demonstration missile manufactured by Shorts in Belfast in their possession. Little denied he was seeking to import guns for Ulster Resistance in exchange for missile technology. He was remanded in custody but was released in October 1991 after being fined and given a suspended sentence.

It would be wrong, of course, to suggest that these strange practices are confined to one section of the Stormont political class. The long-running story relating to the rebuilding of Casement Park Gaelic Athletic Association (GAA) stadium has become something of a cause célèbre. Against the opposition of many local residents, the GAA was awarded a very significant grant by the Sinn Féin Minister for Culture, Arts and Leisure to build a large new stadium in the middle of a residential area.

Critics of the scheme have said that this new stadium is intended as a prestige project for the Sinn Féin party in its West Belfast heartland, presenting tasty photo opportunities for party celebrities attending important football games. Whatever truth there may in these accusations, misfortune and poor planning have bedevilled the project's delivery. The Sinn Féin minister with responsibility, Carál Ní Chuilín, has insisted, nevertheless, on continuing with the project in spite of apparently well-founded criticism from various quarters (*Irish News*, 14 August 2015).

While the same minister was fending off criticism of her handling of the Casement Park case, she was accused of another misjudgement. Her Department of Culture, Arts and Leisure (DCAL) awarded Féile an Phobail a total of £550,000, through a "cultural programme" fund (*BBC News*, 29 October 2015). The recipient of the grant was allowed to disperse a large portion of the fund to other organisations, drawing accusations that the minster was favouring a Sinn Féin voting constituency.

Not every event in Stormont assembly, though, finds Sinn Féin and the DUP publicly critical of each other's effort to find shortcuts to assist their programme. From time to time there are signs of cooperation when the issue is in their mutual self-interest. When Traditional Unionist Voice's Jim Allister attempted legislation to put a cap on special advisers' salaries, Sinn Féin and the DUP combined to defeat the Bill which was supported by all other parties in the Assembly (*Slugger O'Toole*, 13 October 2015).

This situation creates an odd paradox. While Unionist politicians refuse to cooperate with Sinn Féin in public and strive to discomfort it, they have a real interest in keeping that party in the Assembly and hence hold the political institutions in place. On the other hand and odd as it may seem, Sinn Féin is also reluctant to undermine Stormont completely. With one eye on Sinn Fein's plans for southern Ireland, Martin McGuinness is concerned not to undermine the northern institutions and have his party appear "irresponsible or unfit" for government in Dublin.

While the DUP and Sinn Féin would object to being likened with one of the early Christian church saints, there are echoes of the old Saint Augustine in their behaviour. Their reluctance to change is reminiscent of the holy man's prayer, "Lord make me pure but not just yet."[13] Or as a more contemporary observer put it, the pair are staying together for the sake of their MLAs' salaries.

The consequence for working people in the North hardly needs detailing. A malfunctioning political institution

---

13 The DUP praying (à la St Augustine) intone: please Lord rid us of the Shinners but not if it means closing the Assembly with all of those nicely paid positions.

 Sinn Féin praying (à la St Augustine) intone: please Lord deliver us into a united Ireland but would you wait until we have a clear majority of seats in Stormont and Leinster House.

presiding over a malfunctioning political entity that ensures workers remain divided causes endless danger as well as facilitating permanent austerity and the creation of a low-pay economy (see Chapter 2). Northern Ireland already has the lowest average wage in the UK, and current Conservative government plans to cut back on the social welfare safety net are designed to injure the less well-off and force people into minimum-wage jobs. This is set to deepen against the background of fundamental changes to the character of the British welfare state. The agenda for reduction in the welfare spending amounts to more than simply financial reduction and deficit cutting since it is intimately tied to the process of state restructuring more broadly. This is part of a changing United Kingdom in terms of political economy and representative politics. London and the south-east of England are becoming increasingly wealthy and growing apart from the rest of the state. Neo-liberalism has provided the philosophical underpinning for an economic strategy that cares little for the underperforming periphery as the rhetoric about the so-called "northern powerhouse" reveals. The attitude of the May government since Brexit has merely confirmed the shallowness of this rhetoric.

Hence, the objective of cutting the overall welfare budget has to be seen in its wider context where local authorities, and the devolved administrations within the UK state including the Welsh Assembly, the Scottish government and the Northern Ireland Assembly, will be given responsibility without power. This has been described perfectly cogently by Sarah Neville of the *Financial Times*, whose article is worth quoting at length for, amongst other reasons, she cites the unintended irony of the Tory neo-liberal Evangelista – not her term – who have followed the logic – like the money – of their New Labour predecessors:

Under Mr Cameron, public services have adopted an array of approaches, dictated in part by how tough their budgetary allocations have been. Underpinning this is a process known as devolution — a move to decentralise public spending by handing down powers to local bodies, which then have greater freedom over their budgets. Ministers have transferred authority over economic development, policing, education and now local government taxation far more enthusiastically than the Thatcher or Blair governments. Much remains centralised, such as public sector pay, "but on balance it has been a localist austerity programme", Mr Haldenby says. [...] One official in Whitehall describes this as one of the "great bargains of this government: the exchange of power for less money". The changes are also attracting the attention of other cash-strapped nations. (3 December 2015)

We bet they are!
Neville continues,

Dissatisfaction among voters could rise if a move towards more local revenue-raising changes the consensus on which the postwar welfare settlement was built: that all pay into a proportionate tax system to receive common services.

And here's the meat in the sandwich for those believers who think that only those who can pay their way should get their fair share, even though, of course, this only makes sense once ideas of universality are dumped:

More affluent areas will find it easier to raise extra money for amenities such as social care and police. Tax revenue from businesses will also be more plentiful in some places than others, potentially exacerbating patterns of deprivation. John Hills, professor of social policy at the London School of Economics and an expert on the welfare state, suggests this threatens "a trap of the kind that you see with US school funding, where it's locally funded and locally spent and, therefore, a rich area in the US can afford a very good local school and a poor area can't.

And lest austerity is seen as a millstone around the necks of urban working and lower middle classes alone, the outlook for the north's rural communities could hardly be described as rosy. According to reports in the *Belfast Telegraph* (Rutherford 29 January 2016), farming income fell more than forty per cent in twelve months:

> The biggest driver was a fall in dairy prices, which dropped by 27% to £480m. The figures were disclosed in a report published yesterday by the Department of Agriculture and Rural Development. The Ulster Farmers' Union warned it was unlikely to get any better in the months ahead. UFU president Ian Marshall said: "This is a real financial crisis, and it is still there in 2016."

Highlighted was the fact that the crash was so acute that incomes in 2015 had plummeted to £53 million less than Common Agricultural Policy payments. Not good outside the large towns of Belfast and Derry ... not good in rural "Ulster". No one had even factored in the consequences of Brexit.

According to PricewaterhouseCoopers (PwC), growth would be slower in Northern Ireland than in England, Scotland and Wales:

> Northern Ireland's economic progress is likely to continue to lag behind the UK, where output is now well above pre-crash peak, an economist has said. GDP figures from the Office for National Statistics (ONS) showed the UK economy grew by 2.2% last year, down from 2.9% in the previous 12 months. Expansion in the fourth quarter of the year picked up to

0.5% - up from 0.4% in the third quarter and following a rate of 0.5% in the second quarter. [...] The services sector - everything from restaurants to estate agents - was continuing to power the UK recovery, growing 0.7% in the last quarter, the ONS data showed. But production sectors, including manufacturing and oil, were down. (*Belfast Telegraph*, Canning 29 January 2016)

According to Dr Esmond Birnie, PwC chief economist in Northern Ireland, it's going to continue to be pretty bleak.[14] The report concluded by apportioning huge blame for the slowdown in the north on the global economy.

The outcome of the recent round of negotiations in Stormont indicates that self-interest among the political class has caused negotiators to seek the retention of the current status quo: an outcome that does little to improve the lot of the working class whatever their constitutional allegiance may be.

Conclusion: The new convergence

How often have we heard the phrase from Marx's "Eighteenth Brumaire of Louis Napoleon" that "history repeats itself, first as tragedy, then as farce"? That the axiom is overused is hardly surprising since it has been proven accurate so often and rarely more so than when applied to the current administration in Stormont. Once we were afflicted with an uncompromising Unionist regime that governed the six counties with scant regard for democracy and creating misery for many. In its place we now have an administration that appears intent, instead, on making itself a byword for

14 Dr John Esmond Birnie (born 6 January 1965) is an author, economist and Ulster Unionist Party politician. He is also a former Member of the Northern Ireland Assembly (MLA) for South Belfast.

banality and ridicule. The lords Craig and Brookeborough must be turning in their marble tombs as the state they created is now home to what might charitably be described as a political circus.

Ever since the Stormont institutions were restored in 2008 under the management of Sinn Féin and the DUP, there has been growing evidence of the emergence of a Northern Ireland political class. This body of people has been described as a group who, in spite of holding an electoral mandate, simultaneously occupy a world at some distance from many of those they represent.

Moreover, there is also the view in many quarters that while those who hold office in Stormont are not necessarily personally corrupt, they have a vested interest in maintaining the current status quo whether that is for good or ill. More recently it is being argued that, what for a period was a modus vivendi, is now becoming more permanent as, with one exception, many of their core policies converge.

The one and obvious exception to the Stormont consensus is the Nationalist aspiration for an all-Ireland political entity. And it is a Nationalist aspiration as distinct from a republican demand. It has come to be defined by both parties in the Executive as a single jurisdiction issue rather than one providing for a qualitatively different form of governance or economic regime. Nevertheless, since Sinn Féin is content largely to leave the question of an all-Ireland state to the realm of aspiration (albeit with the occasional low-intensity publicity campaign), there are few policy matters to disturb the fundamental stability of the administration or the ongoing coming together of their programmes.

There are of course the raucous squabbles and tantrums that happen frequently but these are never so serious as to undermine the parties' desire to maintain the institutions that provide employment and prestige for the occupants.

From the Stormont Executive's first sitting in 1999 there was a broad acceptance that the region would be administered within the parameters of neo-liberal economics. For example, the Executive's minister for health, Sinn Féin's Barbara de Brun, authorised the closure of the South Tyrone hospital in Dungannon in her first period in office while other members of the administration enthusiastically implemented the Thatcherite policy of public private partnership projects.[15]

There have, nevertheless, been differences between the two main parties as was seen in their responses to the Conservative government's implementation of austerity measures. Both Sinn Féin and the DUP were at first reluctant to agree to the biting cuts and argued that Northern Ireland was a special case in light of the long years of conflict and therefore required additional resources; however, when London refused to accede to their requests, there appeared to be some significant difference between the parties. Sinn Féin refused to sign off on the budget while the DUP appeared to reluctantly acquiesce. The impasse was eventually resolved through providing a Stormont answer to a Stormont dilemma – London was asked (and agreed) to

15 A) "Threatened Hospital Campaign Continues" (BBC News, 28 June 2000)

"... Sinn Fein assembly member Francie Molloy said health minister Bairbre de Brun had promised the hospital would not close and that he believed acute services could be restored to the area. 'I believe the key point is to set up a single management unit for Craigavon and Dungannon hospitals, so that the management unit of Dungannon and Craigavon have total access to the hospitals. Then they will be able to start to put in new services and specialist services, which people currently have to travel to Belfast and other areas to get.'"

B) "Campaigners Lose Hospital Battle" (BBC News, 31 July 2000)

implement the nasty pieces of the austerity package while the Executive got its hands on the less disagreeable parts of the block grant, including the pork-barrel fund.

Although this contretemps appeared to indicate differences, the underlying fact was that no issue was so great that it would force either party to collapse the institutions. This has become still more apparent in the aftermath of the British referendum on EU membership. Indeed the different positions adopted by both parties in relation to the referendum have now been reconciled to an amazing extent.

In August 2016, First Minister Arlene Foster and Deputy First Minister Martin McGuinness wrote a joint letter to British Prime Minister Theresa May. Among other things the letter claims that "EU funds have been hugely important to our economy and the peace process". It then goes on to point out that since 1994 Northern Ireland has received €13 billion and that,

> Our agri-food sector, and hence our wider economy, is therefore uniquely vulnerable both to the loss of EU funding, and to potential tariff and non-tariff barriers to trade.

For an outside observer looking in there would appear to be nothing unusual about this statement, especially since

---

C) "Sinn Fein in Government" (*Irish Marxist Review*, S. McVeigh 2012)

"... From the first days in government Sinn Fein made it clear that it had no problem with privatisation and Private Finance Initiatives. In 2000 when Martin McGuinness was minister for education he announced a new PFI contract to rebuild schools in West Belfast. He said: 'The award of these PFI contracts highlights the opportunities for partnership with the private sector in the pursuit of good value for money and the effective use of resources. It is now clear that PFI does offer real potential for value for money solutions to the pressing capital investment needs of our schools generally.'"

many mainstream economists in Northern Ireland and beyond would heartily endorse the settlement. However, this would be to overlook the fact that less than two months prior to signing the letter, the First Minister had led her party in a campaign to support the Brexit initiative to leave the European Union while Martin's party campaigned for Remain. In spite of Mrs Foster's trenchant denials of having changed direction, it was very clear that this letter heralded a very significant retreat from her stated position prior to 23 June 2016 (EU referendum day).

The DUP U-turn in relation to its views on the European Union had apparently occurred overnight. This would be to overlook the fact that since 2008, the DUP had swallowed hard and kept its constituency within the executive arena with Sinn Féin. Indeed, the party's determination to maintain the political institutions was made very clear by senior party member Sammy Wilson as he commented widely on the fallout from what became known as the Daithí McKay/Jamie Bryson NAMA scandal. It had been discovered that the Sinn Féin MLA had coached a Unionist witness at a hearing that the republican politician had chaired. Yet in spite of this serious breach of protocol, Wilson accepted that the DUP and Sinn Féin would keep on working together.

As a consequence of this mutually shared determination to retain the political institutions in Stormont, political policy accepted by both parties is converging. The DUP is accepting the type of dependency politics coupled with neo-liberalism that is the hallmark of current EU economics. In spite of its strident empire loyalism the party of Ian Paisley has become what the late Margaret Thatcher would have described as "wet".

Simultaneously, Sinn Féin has surrendered any pretence of being a left or socialist organisation. In the same letter signed by Arlene Foster, Sinn Féin's Martin McGuinness reiterated his party's abject acceptance of the neo-imperialist European Union and reinforced his organisation's capitulation to the market by endorsing a call for policies that "need to be sufficiently flexible to allow access to unskilled as well as highly skilled labour". There is no shortage of unskilled labour in Northern Ireland and the insistence on facilitating access to these workers is designed purely to depress the price of labour.

The letter from OFMDFM to Theresa May has effectively sealed the convergence of interests between the two main parties in Stormont. What previously had been a marriage of convenience has now become an uneasy partnership, albeit one with a great number of shared values.

Chapter 5

The Role of the "Third Sector" in Neo-Liberal Northern Ireland

Ever-increasingly, the third sector is becoming a cornerstone of our social infrastructure, supplying vital services to compliment the public sector. When you look at the draft Programme for Government, you see how crucial voluntary and community bodies already are, and will continue to be, to hundreds of thousands of people across Northern Ireland. We need to make explicit what is already obvious to many working in the sector; that leadership of these organisations is making huge efforts to fill the gaps left by public sector funding cuts.

– Majella McCloskey, Chief Executive of CO3[16]

The Housing Executive only turned to the use of private finance (via housing associations) reluctantly, in the absence of sufficient government funding or the option to borrow itself.

– Northern Ireland Council for Voluntary Action (NICVA)[17]

This chapter will look at the role of the "third sector" in Northern Ireland in the context of the hegemonic adherence of the main political parties in Stormont to

16 CO3 is Northern Ireland's umbrella body for third sector chief officers. For more details, see https://www.communityni. org/news/third-sector-enterprises-leading-way-local-management#.v7wxipkrkm8

17 For more details, see http://www.nicva.org/article/double-tranistion-peace-and-neo-liberalism

neo-liberal economic principles and their willingness to sign off on deepening cuts to the public services that had hitherto been widely accepted as a minimal standard of state provision.

As the DUP/SF coalition in Stormont struggles to expound a coherent economic policy in the context of Brexit and a rapidly shrinking public sector in the six counties, neo-liberalism has formulated a simple prescription for the North's "peacetime economy" of swingeing tax cuts for big business, monetisation and privatisation of essential public services, wage depression, and foreign direct investment.

In parallel, one aspect of the third sector in particular – "social enterprise" – has been advanced with both speed and dexterity both in Britain and Ireland since it first appeared in the local social policy lexicon in the mid-1980s. From being part of the domain of enthusiasts for the "social economy", the concept of social enterprise has become widely discussed, increasingly widely written about and, most importantly of all, adopted across UK government policy by both Labour and Tory administrations.

It is important to view the relatively recent growth of the third sector in Northern Ireland in the context not just of post-conflict restructuring of the economy but also of more fundamental developments that are under way in modern European societies. What then is the context for third sector growth? Well firstly, there is the general expansion of the service economy as modern European states change from industrial to post-industrial societies. Secondly, the shift towards a service economy, which benefited the third sector as well, has been reinforced by demographic developments, in particular the generation of baby boomers. In the course of their life cycle, this cohort has brought and will bring long-lasting capacity expansions, including childcare facilities in the 1950s, schools in the 1960s, universities in the 1970s, and homes for the elderly in the 2000s and in the coming decades.

Finally, and most importantly, political and ideological changes since the 1970s have played a significant role in third sector expansion. Specifically, political frameworks and resulting legislatures often decide how existing demand is channelled to the third sector. Many private enterprises and third sector organisations have been tasked with delivering essential services with the help of government funds, and typically as part of complex contracting schemes. There is a deeper ideological reason for the growth of the third sector: the changing role of the state itself. Even though some European countries see themselves in a different ideological tradition, the political currents of both neo-liberalism and Third Way approaches imply a reallocation of responsibilities between state and society. Combined with economic policies that emphasise privatisation of state corporations and holdings, the creeping privatisation of education, health and social security – unthinkable even a few years ago – has now entered the Northern Ireland political lexicon (Anheier 2002).

In an increasingly neo-liberal Europe, the social policy prescriptions of the European Social Democratic compromise have come under a sustained and intense onslaught. The classic welfare state model – "the social contract" adopted as a compromise between capital and labour in the aftermath of the Second World War – is being set aside in many EU member states in favour of a hidden welfare state of tax expenditures, incentives and regulations. This has, in turn, changed the role of the state and its agencies from welfare state guarantor to regulator, grant-giver and public service market maker. This development has had a profound effect on how the contribution of the third sector in Northern Ireland is currently configured and understood by the Stormont administration, by the London government and by think tanks and policymakers in the EU.

Since the 1990s, international financial crises have meant that the ideological discussion around the third sector has become much more politically pragmatic and the overwhelming theme has been the search for alternatives in solving "welfare problems". In the process of outsourcing services from the public sector, the third sector in Northern Ireland has grown to some extent, but the private sector has been a much greater beneficiary. Care of the elderly in the region is a pertinent example of how rapidly government policy has developed a formerly essential public service into a highly profitable income generator for private and third sector entrepreneurs.

The Cabinet Office of the British government until 2010 had an Office of the Third Sector that defined the "third sector" as "the place between State and (the) private sector". The recent Conservative/Liberal Democrat coalition government in Britain renamed the department the Office for Civil Society. The term "third sector" has now largely been replaced in government usage by the term "Civil Society" or more usually the term "Big Society", which was devised by political advisers and which featured prominently in the Conservative Party's 2010 election campaign. The Fresh Start Agreement in Stormont poses no ideological challenge to this political trajectory.

In fact, so embedded has Cameron's "Big Society" lexicography become in the new Northern Ireland that a recently appointed Sinn Féin Lord Mayor proudly pledged to devote his tenure in office to the advancement of "Commerce, Charity and Civic Pride" (*agendaNi*, 18 November 2016). What was envisaged, particularly in Blairite Britain, and with further modification in Cameron's "Big Society" and in May's JAM recipe, was the creation of "new enterprise vehicles" in the UK's most deprived areas. Large third sector charities in Northern Ireland as elsewhere have, for some time, been operating in the mode of very large businesses. They're compelled to; they're bidding against G4S or A4e for the same work; they have to be competitive on price (which is to say, drive down wages in their own organisation) and they have to practise the distinctive discretion of the business world, where all statements are anodyne, because opinions cost customers (and grants) but generate no revenue.

What was being described by Blair, Cameron and May in their adulation of a "Third Way" was, of course, an overt neo-liberal strategy for public service reform and monetisation of vital services including healthcare, education and key utilities – the third sector was being encouraged to adopt a business format and, more significantly, it was being made clear that this approach was likely to be regarded as the prime (if not perhaps the only) source of available government support for the future. Despite the neo-liberal motivation of some of its political advocates, this chapter argues that an economic, political and social space is opening up for the third sector. In addition to traditional non-profit and voluntary organisations, new forms of work and organisations are emerging from the wreckage wrought by neo-liberal doctrine.

A new opposition must be built within the broader "third sector" including the trade union grass roots and independently organised community sector in Northern Ireland. The long-term prognosis for the reformed Northern Ireland is that it will continue to be a failing political and economic entity. The current political arrangements at Stormont remain a bulwark against effective opposition to sectarianism and neo-liberalism. New methods of political education and political activism will be required to break the third sector out of a reliance on lobbying, clientelism and patronage. Above all, the last decade has seen intensely local debates about how wider non-market and common-purpose issues like social justice, the quality of life and the environment are to be dealt with in the context of globalism and neo-liberalism.

In Northern Ireland, there is no simple solution to the question of how social economy organisations can find the most appropriate source of funding, and each avenue has potential political and economic costs associated with it. Whilst some social economy organisations may benefit more from income-generating activities, particularly those who provide goods and services, it may not be an appropriate approach for all social economy organisations. Accordingly, some organisations will be more promiscuous than others in some of their associations with the state and the private sectors.

Social service organisations rely more on government support, while advocacy organisations benefit from philanthropy and self-generated income. Consequently, none of the three main sources (government funding, income-generating activities and philanthropy) are going to provide an effective solution for the sector if considered independently. Continued financing from the EU, Stormont and London administrations might make for the least radical change – provided (and this is the real issue) the choice to rely on this route can be assumed still to exist and can be readily sustained.

Patronage and the third sector

Returning to the local, it should hardly surprise anyone to know that in the sectarian political dispensation of the "New Northern Ireland", third sector funding is open to manipulation and disadvantage criteria are often simply overridden in order to meet the sectarian obligations of the two main sectarian power brokers in government. Further academic research is urgently required to determine how the third sector in Northern Ireland is negotiating the political reciprocity associated with access to local authority, Stormont and EU grant funding. One of the key problems with the enormous increase in statutory funding enjoyed by the third sector in the last twenty years is the way in which it has stripped its beneficiaries of their autonomy and left them vulnerable to changes in government policy. Third sector organisations which rely on the government for seventy five to one hundred per cent of their income cannot call themselves independent in any meaningful sense. Many organisations acknowledge this, but the kind of funding they say would give them greater independence – unrestricted grants – is evidently not conducive to transparency and accountability.

State-funded organisations in the third sector in Northern Ireland who remain silent about the inequitable outcomes of social and economic policies emanating from the DUP/SF coalition are susceptible to allegations of colluding with the state. If by that we mean "cooperation" or "collaboration", then that is exactly what politicians expect when they employ the third sector to assist in the delivery of their socio-economic prescriptions. It is what anybody expects when they exchange money for services. When politicians spend public money to achieve political objectives, it is naive to think that politics doesn't matter.

The DUP/SF administration is certainly under no obligation to fund any third sector group and if a local third sector organisation dislikes the ruling parties enough to be briefing journalists and undermining policies, the current coalition might consider it to be in its best interests to direct its Westminster allocation away from malcontents (too often maligned and misrepresented as "enemies of the peace process") and towards groups which remain "on message", or at least neutral, in respect of the political project of the two main parties. Therein lays the third sector's fundamental rationale for self-censorship, conservatism, conformity and compliance in the face of a political dispensation intent on delivering neo-liberal and sectarian remedies for Northern Ireland's terminally ailing economy.

The question then for the Stormont Executive is whether to continue funding groups which do not share their political and economic vision (whatever that may be), while the question for the "sock puppet" organisations in the third sector is whether to keep quiet and hope the funding rug is not pulled out from under them. Those who benefit from political patronage are, therefore, highly vulnerable to changes of government direction in both Westminster and Stormont. The UK Panel on the Independence of the Voluntary Sector, chaired by the former head of Barnardo's, Sir Roger Singleton, had as its central message, "A charity sector reliant on government contracts would find it difficult to criticise government policy" (*Guardian*, 22 January 2013).

Often, loyalty and non-dissension are dictated by explicit gagging orders in government contracts. It's not a matter of discretion; it's a matter of law. Other times, social economy organisations self-censor on the basis that this dance never ends – they will always be bidding for new contracts and funds. The need to be viewed favourably by a particular government department or the relevant "super council" will never go away. This is a high-stakes game for the third sector. During the 2007–2013 planning period, Northern Ireland had a range of programmes to promote economic and social progress and peace and reconciliation. Between 1995 and 2015 in terms of PEACE programmes alone, this amounted to considerable sums of financial support (European Commission, 2014; 2018). (PEACE has been extended until 2020 "with a strong emphasis on children and young people", 2018). As the commission pointed out in 2008,

> There has been long-standing EU financial support for Northern Ireland as one of the priority "Objective 1" regions. In the period 2000-2006, the six programmes (including the "Building Sustainable Prosperity" and the PEACE II programme) received EU aid of some EUR 2.2 billion to which was added the EU contribution to the International

Fund for Ireland. One of the innovative features of EU cohesion policy in Northern Ireland has been the PEACE programme, first established in 1995, specifically targeted on support for joint projects of a socio-economic nature with the view to assisting peace and reconciliation between the two communities. For the current planning period, 2007-2013, Northern Ireland has 6 programmes with a financial contribution of EUR 1.1 billion, including a continuation of the PEACE programme. (European Commission 2008)

The selective dispersal of EU funds to Northern Ireland since the 1980s has done much to isolate and marginalise third sector organisations whose public pronouncements have not chimed with the state-sponsored narrative of the peace process and the parallel neo-liberal economic settlement overseen by Washington and London. Of course, state patronage is nothing new. James Craig, the first prime minister of Northern Ireland after partition, described government as a matter of "distributing bones". In the sectarian blocs that were embedded in the two states established after partition in Ireland – and which were reinforced in the sectarian settlement of the GFA in 1998 – the politics of patronage have displaced the modernisation associated more widely across Western Europe with the expansion of the franchise, expressed in the definition of politics along left-right lines. Political patronage in Northern Ireland has guaranteed that civic and class identity continue to be trumped by ethnic tribalism.

A new approach to achieve maximum, strategic political impact (which translates into party political advantage) from funding was introduced in Northern Ireland in 2007. Local councils dominated by Sinn Féin and the DUP formed eight clusters composed of elected representatives, "social partners" and statutory representatives that play a strategic part in the delivery of EU "PEACE funding". Peppered with political apparatchiks posing as "community development workers", they have developed local "peace and reconciliation action plans" to distribute the bones to political sympathisers and thereby consolidate support based on sectarian patronage. Overall management of the programme is handled by the Special EU Programmes Body. This body is supervised by a monitoring committee whose members represent the main political interest groups in Northern Ireland and the border regions of Ireland.

In light of such blatant sectarian patronage and in the absence of a significant parliamentary or indeed extra-parliamentary opposition movement at Stormont, the announcement of the latest rewriting of the GFA, the ironically entitled "Fresh Start", was met by a wave of public apathy and indifference. There were a number of reasons for ordinary citizens' disinterest. High levels of corruption and sectarianism, coupled with almost absolute impunity even when corruption is exposed, have led many workers to regard the local administration in Stormont with ill-concealed contempt.

The decision in October 2016 by the DUP/SF coalition to channel a £1.7 million investment in East Belfast through a group linked to the UDA is but the latest in a series of politically motivated disbursements of public monies and largesse for party political advantage. In a not unrelated development, recent political advances in East Belfast by the moderate unionist Alliance Party were met with DUP smear campaigns and Unionist paramilitary threats and intimidation towards leading Alliance Party representatives.

UDA boss Jimmy Birch and close associate Dee Stitt both hold senior positions in Charter NI which the Northern Ireland Executive Office has hand-picked to manage the massive investment of public money. Birch sits on the UDA-linked group's board of directors while convicted gunman Stitt is its chief executive. Announcing Charter NI's involvement at a press conference, DUP

First Minister Arlene Foster said, "This project is exactly what the Social Investment Fund is all about." The First Minister was pictured standing beside Stitt (*Irish News*, 30 September 2016).

On the other side of the sectarian playing field, the same fund has been used to bolster political support for Sinn Féin in Nationalist areas of Northern Ireland where their rivals for sectarian political support in the SDLP still retain a significant support base. Community organisations, GAA football clubs and capital projects closely associated with Sinn Féin representatives and activists, either directly, through family connections or through business sponsorship, have been earmarked for millions in public funding via the notorious and nakedly sectarian SIF initiative in order to shore up flagging electoral support in targeted constituencies.

Sinn Féin apparatchiks have also become adept in the formation of third sector organisations that conceal party representatives' interests in agencies that draw down government funding and tax payers' monies. The infamous cases of the Tyrone Cultural Association and Research Services Ireland, though several years apart, are reflective of a deepening culture of contempt for standards in public life and accountability to voters (*Irish News*, 23 November 2016; *BBC News*, 26 November 2014).

It is clear to all but the wilfully blind that the GFA and its subsequent amendments, while currently containing levels of political and sectarian violence, have economically failed the working people of Northern Ireland, and each subsequent political agreement has in turn increasingly secured the interests of neo-liberalism on both sides of the Irish Sea and the Irish border. The economy and therefore the social and material basis of people's lives are becoming more and more precarious and remote.

In response to the growing marginalisation from the centres of decision-making that so directly affect working-class people's lives, the relationship between civic society, Stormont, London, Dublin and Brussels is coming into increasingly stark relief. The revolt of large sections of the working class during the recent EU Referendum in the UK is evidence that the thinly disguised class war politics of austerity may eventually have awakened sections of the population to the reality of neo-liberalism's destructive agenda. This latter message has sent the sectarian parties in Northern Ireland into confused rantings about democratic accountability and political realignments.

Post EU Referendum, the DUP and Sinn Féin have both been vocal in their calls for abrogation of political sovereignty away from citizens of the north and for continued loyalty towards the political and economic elites of London and Brussels respectively. Neither party makes little or any effort to hide the system of political patronage at play in the distribution of European and Westminster funding. The fact that no significant challenge yet appears to be emerging to the current set-up in the north breeds further resignation and disillusionment. Any discussion of an alternative within local civic society has been marginalised by the establishment and corporate media who have, by and large, failed to turn the microscope on the system of patronage that sustains the so-called "peace process" and the local political institutions.

On economic policy there is broad agreement between the two largest parties in Northern Ireland. The overall thrust of their limited political sovereignty is to significantly reduce the state sector and to increase the role of private companies and the third sector in the delivery of public services. A singular example of Sinn Féin and the DUP's shared objectives emerged in the financial monitoring round in the wake of the Fresh Start Agreement. Both parties jointly announced that £48 million would be allocated to the Department of Health in order to reduce waiting lists. This will be used to pay for procedures not through the

NHS, but through private healthcare providers – referred to by the former Minister for Health, appointed after the 2016 election, Michelle O'Neill, now leader of Sinn Féin in the Assembly, as "the independent sector" (*News Letter*, 7 June 2016).

Advocates for the social economy have emphasised the potential for third sector organisations to act as conduits for greater participation and democratic engagement. This is more than simply fostering social inclusion; rather it is a way of empowering individuals who, for a variety of reasons, have been excluded and marginalised. In the face of current trends towards the hegemony of market forces, it might have been anticipated that it would be more difficult to hold on to those values that privilege common purpose, cooperation and solidarity (i.e. those that characterise social economy approaches) over individualism, meritocracy and competitive rivalry. But an argument can also be employed in reverse – that these are precisely the circumstances under which social and moral values are most likely to be re-evaluated and reasserted.

From a left political perspective, some social economy organisations have proven to be successful in promoting new forms of local democratic participation and empowerment, owing to their capacity to contribute to a participatory democracy wherein citizens can actively express their commitment to economic and social development and civic life in their area. Small regional examples of worker cooperatives and other progressive forms of democratic economic organisation already exist in Belfast, Derry and other municipal centres in the north. There are some identifiable common characteristics that could enable the third sector in Northern Ireland to act as potentially independent, non-governmental agencies that have an ambition to create a different sort of economy – one that has a different approach to the organisation of work and production and the distribution of surplus.

For their part, right-wing political ideologues argue that there is a need for alternatives to the state and public sector in general and that non-profit could be one option. Others on the left see the social economy in the contemporary world as a Trojan horse facilitating the marketisation of the social realm – that is, the penetration of what was traditionally the sphere of publicly delivered public services and the third sector by market-based forms of contracting and exchange. In short, the existence of non-profit organisations can usually be traced back to the presence of market and state failures in satisfying the demands of social and collective interests, within the criteria of reasonable cost and quality. The fact remains that the genuine social economy, as originally perceived, is an alternative ideology that privileges solidaristic working, social and distributive justice, and quality of life and the environment over the demands of the free market. It is at least, in a world of dominant neo-liberal ideology, a place where such debates can continue to take place.

How the Northern Ireland administration defines the social economy will have important consequences for the way in which social economy organisations function in the period ahead, and the resources which are made available to them. Since the funders for a significant part of the social economy are governments, it might be argued that there is no effective radicalism at work here – just an alternative (third) way of marshalling new social forms to find solutions to pressing problems. Where, however, there is more evidence of room for radical or alternative intent is that the social economy brings into play issues around poverty, social exclusion, economic participation, democratic engagement, inequality, empowerment etc. Despite the narrow instrumental objectives that define their grant-funded actions, most of the organisations currently structured within the social economy are drawn in, by definition, to uphold values that privilege a democratic and inclusive approach and social values over individualism and market forces.

It all sounds both straightforward and inevitable – whether by contract or grant, most of the third sector will always be part-funded by the state. Funded organisations will never be in a great position to bite the hand that feeds them, so they should leave the hand-biting to other organisations, i.e. social economy organisations that don't bid for contracts and can therefore afford to be inflammatory. With sufficient will, resourcefulness, imagination and creativity, actors within the social economy can still find the flexibility and freedom to challenge orthodox and hierarchical work-management structures and create space even within the present economic system for notions of advocacy, solidarity, democracy and alternative ways of looking at the interplay between work, society and the political economy.

Chapter 6

On the Psychology of War and Conflict in the North

The madness of war

While universal mental healthcare models will necessarily have traction in cities such as Birmingham, Liverpool, London and Cardiff, Northern Ireland has historically unique problems requiring specific therapeutic responses. Despite the devastation wrought by the forty-year conflict, including persistent mental trauma, and high suicide rates and levels of addiction, there have been limited attempts to develop a model of care to meet the needs of the people who experienced war. Given the recognition of the social roots of mental health problems and especially in a so-called post-conflict society, it is disturbing that so many conflict-generated problems are regarded as if they can be treated in a "normal" way. Then again, given that the state, in its "normalisation of civil insurgency" mode, treated the conflict as one of good guys versus bad guys, of cops and robbers, it should probably come as no surprise that those suffering from its effects should be denied conflict-specific treatments. Their suffering has nothing to do with the war (what war was that?) and everything to do with the pathologies of everyday, contemporary life.

Would that it were so, though that would be bad enough for sure. This chapter principally provides a narrative of the experience of trauma as recounted by a defined group of patients living in a part of West Belfast. While far from attempting to represent anything more than a small sample, it nevertheless helps to shine some light on the connection between the past conflict in the North and contemporary personal traumas. Not all psychological problems in the north are reducible to "typical" everyday pathologies – whatever "typical" and "everyday" might mean, though we know these words can often act as a means to buffer things from their historical roots. Until the state recognises the role of the long war in the presentation of many contemporary emotional and psychological problems, misrecognition at best, or denial at worst, of many emotional difficulties and psychological distress will continue. At the very least, we need to recognise that the war, the emotional and psychological war, is not over, has never ended for many. But there is another aspect to the persistence of post-war trauma too: its trans-generational reproduction in the mental (and thus material) lives of many.

It is difficult to overstate the extent to which transgenerational trauma remains unacknowledged in the post-war generation in the North. There has been a rise in drug misuse in towns and cities across Northern Ireland. Recently a GP from West Belfast, cited in the *Irish News*, stated that West Belfast had reached unprecedented heroin addiction levels:

> Dr Michael McKenna, who is based in the mid-Falls area, said three addicts - all men - attending his practice had died in the past year, while a woman with a heroin dependency died in 2014. All were under the age of 30, and one was a non-national. Previously most addicts and heroin-related deaths had been confined to north Antrim, with a high-profile community addiction unit based in Ballymena. (15 February 2016)

This was exceptional in Dr McKenna's experience. He said that in West Belfast deaths resulting from heroin were "completely unheard of" and that, "We are also seeing a big rise in the number young women who have drug dependencies, with heroin among the drugs" (ibid.). Arguably, the extent of drug misuse suggests that essentially young people are self-medicating. Having drifted through the social work and mental healthcare system, many are now filing the so-called social justice system.

The central question for anyone concerned with a progressive agenda that seeks to go beyond the previous civil conflict is to begin from the recognition that much of the identified trauma has conflict-specific legacies. In that case we need to ask why it is that policymakers are not looking at these glaring facts. One instance where we can see a glimmer of light is in Derry where the independent candidate (for Derry City and Strabane Council), Dee Quigley, was elected on a campaign to deliver a drug addiction treatment centre.

It is vital therefore that other progressive candidates address this concern, indeed seeking to make it a priority. It's not obvious that government actors understand the relationship between self-empowerment and political action – that getting people off drugs can be the precursor to a different kind of (non-sectarian) politics here. That practical, therapeutic treatment is itself political because it can be the beginning of a process of political action. This is another way of saying that challenging drugs and the processes of disenfranchisement linked to emotional and psychological repression is also the territory we need to find to create a new anti-sectarian agenda, a new politics. Democracy and engagement are a fiction while so many people are on heroine and prescribed pharmaceuticals. We need to push for treatment and preventative healthcare models as opposed to the existing reactive models that have been proven to be singularly ineffective.

For example, in case of the need to be convinced at the paucity of the current approach separating the recent conflict from mental health issues here, the healthcare trusts in Northern Ireland spend millions sending young people to England. People diagnosed with "Personality Disorder" (sometimes even "eating disorders") are sent to expert treatment units in England because there are no services anywhere here, or in the Republic, offering specialist support – that is, unless by "specialist" one means prison and secure units. Our young working class will continue to be failed by us, by the "war generation", while this abandonment continues.

The following is taken, by kind permission, from the published work of a community psychiatric nurse who practised in a part of West Belfast during the early years after the signing of the GFA.[18]

I have worked as a mental health nurse for 30 years, and I spent 10 of those years working in North and West Belfast. Between 1969 and 1998, Northern Ireland suffered 30 years of war. Approximately 3,600 deaths and 40,000 severe injuries resulted from this war which is commonly referred to as "the troubles". The impact of the war was not uniform across Northern Ireland. Over 25 per cent of deaths occurred in North and West Belfast.

Post-war research in mental health is generally limited to symptoms of Post-Traumatic Stress Disorder (PTSD). However, I have seen how exposure to war can cause other forms of severe, complex, and enduring mental illnesses.

The unacknowledged role of war in these illnesses combines with disdain shown to those who were imprisoned, tortured, or part of the resistance to Britain's role in the war. Their disabilities are treated as personal defects, not as the

18   The patients' stories recounted here were first presented in an original paper, written by Patricia Campbell, Maneesh Gupta and Elizabeth Schumacher, titled "Mental Health Symptoms Post Conflict: A Case Series from West Belfast, Northern Ireland" (2009). The paper is as-yet unpublished, but is available from the authors upon request.

result of war trauma. Failure to understand the role of the war in mental illness leads to less effective treatment, social isolation, worsening symptoms, and a destructive effect on the subsequent generation.

The following five patients, who were directly exposed to military conflict in West Belfast, provided consent for their stories to be recorded. Their names are fictitious.

(Note: All non-state military armed groups are described as "paramilitary".)

Sean

Sean is a 58-year-old man who lives alone. During all 30 years of the conflict, he worked for the local government in West Belfast. He was targeted as a council worker, facing resistance from all sides, and he was regularly stopped and interrogated.

Every day, Sean negotiated blockades, barricades, and burning vehicles. He witnessed shootings and killings and retrieved dead bodies from the street. He was subject to ambushes and weekly army house raids at all times of the day and night. One day, his house was raided three times. He narrowly survived when paramilitaries entered his work premises and opened fire with a machine gun, killing two co-workers and injuring five others, including him.

While in custody, Sean witnessed torture and was himself tortured with sleep deprivation and beatings. One time, the soldier to whom he was handcuffed apologized for what he was about to do, explaining that he had only nine days left before he was out of the army.

Sean shuns personal relationships for fear of "getting too close". He has a history of alcohol dependence, depressed moods, interpersonal difficulties, and hyper-vigilance. He overeats and is obese. He was treated with an antidepressant and psychotherapy/trauma therapy.

Barry

Barry is a 50-year-old man who lives alone. At age 14, he recalls seeing his brother shot at by the army and then being driven over by an armoured vehicle. He described his brother's head "bursting" and the contents of his head "spraying the wall". He later cleaned parts of his brother's brain from the wall.

At age 16, Barry was imprisoned in Long Kesh and was there during the burning and gassing of the prison. He described his life as constantly under threat and felt the need to "always be on the move".

At age 18, Barry was imprisoned in the H Blocks of Long Kesh, then released and re-arrested at age 24 for possession of explosives. During this period he had his first "breakdown". He was moved to the prison hospital where he was diagnosed with Schizophrenia at age 28.

Barry still feels unsafe, and he sleeps on the sofa in his living room. He is socially isolated. Some of his friends were killed during the war or later completed suicide as a result of the war. He has tried to end his own life on a number of occasions, the most recent being the previous year when he attempted to hang himself.

Barry is fixated on the "suffering of children in the Middle East". He is obsessed with God and often believes that other people are God. He was prescribed two antipsychotics – an oral medication and a biweekly injection.

Eamon

Eamon is a 51-year-old man who lives with his wife and family. During the war, he was subject to house raids, and he witnessed shootings and killings. He was imprisoned in the H block during the 10-year hunger strike. He was part of the "blanket" protests and "dirty" protests of 1980s. During this time he reported daily torture – strip searches, forced anal searches, and general humiliation and dehumanisation.

Eamon has a history of alcohol dependence and hallucinations that order him to kill. He has visions of stabbing people and killing animals. He suffers depressed moods and insomnia. He was prescribed an antipsychotic, an antidepressant, and a sedative.

Fergus

Fergus is a 56-year-old man who lives with his wife. He reports repeated house raids by police and British soldiers throughout the period of conflict. One time, when his house was invaded by armed and masked paramilitaries, he was imprisoned upstairs and forced to listen to the screams of his son who was being beaten.

Fergus worked as a taxi driver and was hijacked on three occasions during the course of his taxiing duties. The first time, he was held captive while his taxi was used to transfer a bomb. The second time, he was forced to drive a bomb through the local area to a police station. He saw children in the streets and was terrified that the bomb would explode. The third time, he was called to what he thought was a routine taxi duty, but instead he was forced to a take paramilitaries to a shooting against the opposition forces. After this he was arrested and interrogated. The interrogators threatened to release his details to the opposing paramilitaries, and he has lived in fear of retribution ever since.

Fergus's first mental breakdown was in 1994. He reports that his personality changed, and he became introverted, suicidal, and blackened the house windows. He had several hospital admissions, and he attempted suicide via overdose on three different occasions. One time, he threw himself in front of a car and severely injured his hand.

Fergus sleeps in his day clothes and is alcohol dependent. He is depressed and hyper-vigilant. Both his brother and cousin were killed during the conflict. He has a difficult personal relationship with wife who also suffers with depression. He is an amputee and also suffers from angina, diabetes, insomnia, and arthritis. He was prescribed two antipsychotics, an antidepressant, and two sedatives.

Tomas

Tomas is a 54-year-old man who lives alone. In the early 1970s, his father was killed by paramilitaries, and he had to identify the body. Shortly afterwards he was wounded by paratroopers.

Tomas witnessed his friend being shot in the neck and killed. He described the room being full of blood with the smell of burning flesh. Tomas was subject to frequent house raids and detentions. He slept on his sofa during the war because he was afraid of being shot in his bed.

Tomas is dependent on alcohol and suffers auditory hallucinations. He thinks there are microphones coming out of the walls and that his home is "bugged" by the British. He suffers the olfactory hallucination of burning flesh and the visual hallucination of blood on the floor. He remains hyper-vigilant and still sleeps on the sofa so he will be prepared for an attack or house raid. He was prescribed two antipsychotics, an antidepressant, and a sedative.

Treatment

All of our patients were prescribed psychotropic medications – combinations of antipsychotics, antidepressants and sedatives (anxiolytics and hypnotics). High doses of medication, combination treatments, and the offer of therapy have not made a substantial difference in their functioning. Patients do not respond to the available treatments, and they self-medicate.

Most of our patients refuse therapy. Like most traumatised people, they do not want to revisit their traumatic experiences. However, there is another reason; these veterans had been condemned, ostracised and silenced, especially by the Church and the media, so they have difficulty trusting service providers to sympathize with their suffering. As one patient said, "that doctor is the only doctor who recognises that I fought in a war".

Patients cannot develop a therapeutic relationship with those who only treat their symptoms and disregard the source of their wounds. Rather than subject themselves to that humiliation, they prefer to self-medicate. All of our patients used alcohol to numb their pain.

People who have been traumatised by war need more than drugs; they need complex interventions. Group therapy can help veterans express how the war has affected them. The tradition of *testamonio* – sharing stories in a supportive environment – can help participants view their problems, not as personal failings, but as the collective wounds of war. The recognition of shared experiences can alleviate symptoms and promote a sense of belonging, acceptance, and validation.

There is no funding for socially supportive therapies, especially not for therapies that politicize what the system prefers to treat as individual problems. Patient isolation is reinforced by the dismantling of our health services. Austerity policies are ripping the social safety net out from under the most vulnerable. Instead of investing in caring for people who suffered decades of war and deprivation, money is being squandered on executive pay and questionable excessive expenses.

Conclusion

- Armed conflict creates inescapable danger, helplessness, and terror for entire populations. When wars end, economic domination may well intensify, imposing injurious working conditions, high unemployment, and poverty. Chronic mental illness, including psychosis, is subsequently high in such areas.

- The psychological impact of war extends into the future as children develop in an environment saturated with the previous generation's unspoken pain, anger and loss.

- Suicide has become a major problem in Northern Ireland for those who experienced the conflict and for their children. Since 1998, the year the GFA was signed, the number of suicides has continued to climb to a shocking level although a slight fall in the rate was registered in 2014.

- "Northern Ireland continues to have the highest rate of suicide in the UK, per head of population, according to the Office for National Statistics (ONS). The [...] figures show that during 2014 there were 16.5 suicides per 100,000 in Northern Ireland. Scotland had the second highest rate, at 14.5, followed by 10.3 in England and 9.2 in Wales. It is the second consecutive year that Northern Ireland has recorded the UK's highest suicide rate" (*BBC News*, 4 February 2016). While there was a small drop in the rate for Northern Ireland, "This reflected a small decrease in the total number of suicides across the UK as a whole in 2014, where the overall figure fell by 2%."

- While policymakers emphasise suicide prevention and suicide awareness, they ignore the social causes of suicide – the continuing misery of social and economic deprivation.

- The highly publicised "peace process" implied that the war in Northern Ireland was over and everything was resolved. In reality, the war never ended; it simply shifted from military to economic, and sectarian strife continues.

- West Belfast has the highest rates of unemployment and child poverty in the United Kingdom. It is the most socially and economically deprived area in Western Europe.

- In West Belfast, heroin addiction has reached unprecedented levels. Addiction to this powerful painkiller is not surprising in a population that is filled with pain. And those who see no future are understandably angry. In the most disadvantaged areas, angry young people gather and engage in intimidating behaviour. As politicians call for tougher sentences for youth, jails and prisons fill with the children of the war.

- As long as war dominates society, mental illness will increase. Healthcare workers can promote mental health by acknowledging the societal roots of mental illness.

- We must do more than manage the misery that war creates. We must organise to dismantle the war machine.

Chapter 7

Trade Unionism in the North

Over many years the trade union movement in Northern Ireland has struggled to cope with the ever-present difficulties posed by a workforce divided along politically sectarian lines. For several decades after the northern state was founded, the pro-Unionist working class enjoyed some measurable, albeit modest, benefits in terms of employment. They benefited through privileged access to available jobs, and this advantage was reinforced by a state which provided financial incentives to those who invested in pro-Unionist areas.

As a consequence, trade union density was much greater within the Unionist working class than within their Nationalist neighbours for the simple reason that Unionist workers made up the majority of those with a unionised job. Trade union organisers and officials were therefore faced with the awkward reality that the majority of their members were strong supporters of the Northern Ireland state and all that that entailed.

In spite of these inauspicious circumstances, the trade union movement in Northern Ireland managed to remain intact throughout the decades. This was not achieved without difficulties and setbacks and compromises, but some notable successes have to be acknowledged. By deliberately fudging several serious issues, Northern Irish trade unionism remained part of the all-Ireland body and therefore avoided the pitfall of reinforcing sectarian divisions by creating the potential of an Ulster TUC for Protestant workers and an ICTU (Irish Congress of Trade Unions) for Catholic workers. Throughout the most recent conflict, the Northern Ireland Committee of the ICTU (NIC-ICTU) put a priority on remaining intact at the expense of taking any radical action and in some ways this decision was understandable in the circumstances.

Unfortunately this now appears to have created a mindset that rejects any and every form of radical action that might possibly discomfort the local devolved administration in Stormont. Having originally publicised its objections to acceptance of the so-called austerity measures being demanded by the Tory government in London, the NIC-ICTU did a spectacular U-turn when the Stormont administration accepted the package known as Fresh Start.

Justifying Congress's decision in an interview with the Belfast-based newspaper the *Irish News*, ICTU general secretary Peter Bunting said, "We looked into an abyss and we withdrew from the abyss because the inevitability of having a major oppositional campaign against our own politicians was catastrophic in the long term for us" (*Irish News*, 16 December 2015).

While the trade union leader struggled manfully to describe this capitulation as a decision based on hard-headed pragmatism, it is difficult to avoid the conclusion that it was in fact abject surrender. The Fresh Start document had detailed the extent of the cutbacks in place, not the least of which was the making of 20,000 public sector workers redundant over the coming decade.

Interestingly, Peter Bunting's views were not universally shared across the trade union movement in Northern Ireland. The Northern Ireland Public Service Alliance (NIPSA) union's general secretary designate Alison Millar said at the time that the Fresh Start deal did nothing for the union's members, the north's citizens or the region's public services. Nor was Millar alone in her view since members of Unite the Union's community branches also publicly voiced their discontent.

Indeed Unite has played a significant part in changing the attitude of the trade union movement in Ireland over the past few years. In the Republic of Ireland, Unite played a central role in promoting trade union involvement in the Right2Water campaign to prevent the introduction of water charges. This movement drew tens of thousands into political activity and has influenced a significant change in the shape of politics in that part of Ireland.

Admittedly, the Right2Water struggle was focused on the southern Irish state and moreover, was not endorsed by all sections of organised labour in the Republic. At the movement's biannual conference in Ennis in 2015, Unite proposed and won a motion calling on the ICTU to oppose water charges (*Irish Times*, 8 July 2015). The margin of victory was slim – 203 to 194 – and reflected to a certain extent the temper of working people in Ireland. The Irish trade union movement is an island-wide organisation and the motion was carried thanks to drawing crucial support from some senior officials among the northern area's representatives.

Challenges for trade unions in a neo-liberal world – the danger in clutching at straws

One difficulty is that even where labour movement criticisms of supine positions of the sort taken by, for example Bunting, are clear and explicit in their rejection of cuts to public services, some of those making the criticisms may need to take a closer look at the agenda they commit to. In so many respects it is not difficult to see why trade union leaders may sometimes end up in the contradictory position of advocating policies while attacking others within the movement for embracing the very same policies. We live in desperate times where the labour movement, devoid of alternatives, can be seen clutching eagerly at virtually any hope of salvation, even when the only thing being saved is the skin of neo-liberal social and economic policies. As we have been arguing throughout, the neo-liberal agenda embraced by the leading Orange-Green coalition parties in Stormont is not to be understood as a simple policy device that can be easily cast aside once embraced – or, it can, but not without a radical transformation of ideas. This is for the reason, simply put, that neo-liberalism is an all-embracing philosophy. This does not mean that everyone agrees with it nor even that those implementing it necessarily agree with it since as often as not, the very neo-liberal agenda they are supporting is presented as completely the opposite of neo-liberalism: a wolf in sheep's clothing.

It might well be the case, as with the example we give below of the Bengoa proposals for health service reform, that trade union leaders actually deliver on a neo-liberal agenda even while at the same time arguing that they are vehemently opposed to it. This is because, as exponents of a hegemonic philosophy, those committed to neo-liberal marketisation set an agenda that is persuasive to the extent that trade unionists believe what they are doing is open and democratic and even, dare we say it, democratically better than what is currently on offer. A neo-liberal agenda is presented, sweetened in its way, as its opposite. We can see this with the case of the Bengoa report into health service reform.[19] NIPSA, at the forefront of labour movement criticism of Bunting and the NIC-ICTU, have embraced with open arms the Bengoa report.

Connla Young, writing in *Irish News* (5 February 2016), considered the question of criticisms of the trade unions over attitudes to Fresh Start. She highlighted the fact that,

> A Prominent member of the north's largest trade union has called on leading members of the movement to reject the Fresh Start political deal or consider resigning. Senior Nipsa member Padraig Mulholland made the dramatic call after Irish Congress of Trade Unions (ICTU) assistant general secretary Peter Bunting faced unprecedented calls to resign from members of his own movement.

19 The full Bengoa report is available at https://www.ncbi.nlm.nih.gov/pmc/articles/PMC3812354/

In her article Young pointed out that,

> Mr Bunting has previously said that, while ICTU has
> backed the deal, it remains opposed to welfare reform and
> other cuts. As well as being a Nipsa general council member,
> Mr Mulholland is a leading figure in the powerful Broad Left
> grouping within the union. Mr Mulholland described the
> ICTU position as 'disgraceful'.

Young quotes Mulholland as saying,

> In Nipsa we are opposed to the Fresh Start agreement and
> more specifically we are opposed to the position adopted
> by the ICTU. [...] We are shocked by it and we believe it
> to be a disgraceful position for the union movement to be
> in. [...] ICTU'S leadership has put the interests of political
> representatives in Stormont above the members of the
> workplace. [...] We want to see the trade union movement
> getting off its knees, standing up for members and taking on
> the Northern Ireland assembly.

How can this be the case? A brief examination into the
way the Bengoa report has been presented might help to
shed some light on why a number of leaders in the trade
union movement have embraced it so enthusiastically.
Some context is necessary here.

There were four reviews prior to the Bengoa report: Hayes
2001 recommended the removal of A&E services from
smaller hospitals; the Bamford Review 2003 and Compton
2011 both recommended the reduction of acute hospitals;
and Donaldson 2014 recommended a further reduction of
acute hospital services. Essentially, each review, costing the
taxpayer copious sums of public money, focused on cutting
services. The Bengoa report is a ten-year plan and is in the
process of being implemented. Of huge concern is the fact
that the unions in the public sector are in support of what

the then health minister, Michelle O'Neill, described as "a foundation for my vision".

Professor Bengoa is a globally recognised expert in healthcare reform; a former health minister in the Basque region, he has advised the European Union and the Obama administration. In addition to a range of problems we outline herein, arguably the most significant is the absence of any real recognition of our special status, including the mental health needs and implications of the long period of civil conflict. There is no acknowledgement that failure to invest in healthcare and social models must be challenged if the needs of our people are to be met.

In a radio interview, Bengoa outlined his vision for implementation, making the argument that "the solution is at the periphery" (BBC Radio Ulster, 16 October 2016). He advocated a bottom-up implementation with a top-down approach. In his view clinical experts must be central to the running of the system, including the appointment of regional officers with the "technical and political know how [...] to be politically and technically respected by nurses and doctors" (ibid.). We read into this the fact that regional officers will be from the main parties: a DUP-Sinn Féin-run health service.

It is easy to see, if one wants to see things through Bengoa's rose-tinted spectacles, that the language suggesting self-management and direct democracy from below means exactly that – something warm and progressive for all those seeking a riposte to neo-liberalism's top-down instrumental agendas. Self-management by workers who make the service work! The reality is however that decisions will be taken from on high with consultation to follow. There are two types of consultation in our view. The first is consultation on an equal basis – real partnership. The second is the usual top-down approach where decisions are made and consultation follows: that is, consultation about how to implement the top-down decisions, and it is this approach that is applicable in the case of the Bengoa report. It is a top-down, centralised control model, dressed up as a partnership with the people. Moreover, so far as it is "bottom-up", it is only really from the bottom of managerial-level decision-making. The fact is that the health service in Northern Ireland is the largest employer here and the report will see significant changes to workers' terms and conditions. In this respect workers' rights will be compromised in such a way as to a have major impact upon labour market and employment standards more broadly in the north. The idea that the public health sector represents the "good employer" will take another blow and will be well received by privatisers everywhere in the north. This means that the response by the labour movement is vital in challenging a marketising neo-liberal agenda of cuts to our publicly funded health service. Let's now turn to the reaction by some in the trade union movement to Bunting and NICTU's warm response to Fresh Start, so roundly criticised by NIPSA.

The trade union response to Bengoa

Kevin McCabe, NIPSA Assistant Secretary with responsibility for the health sector, welcomed the Bengoa report but said it requires further detailed analysis, though how a report that requires further analysis might be so genially received leaves us perplexed. McCabe stated,

> There are elements we can embrace such as the recommendation that there should be coordinated workforce and service planning carried out on the basis of the population's need rather than with the aim of maintaining services which are not sustainable in the long term. (*ITV News*, 25 October 2016)

Our reading of this is that he is accepting the argument for cuts on the basis that services are not sustainable.

> A major short term issue for the Minister to resolve is the elective care issue whilst the acid test for the NI Executive is the commitment to seek additional resources for Northern Ireland to fund the change programme. (Ibid.)

For McCabe, union members "for too long" have faced failed attempts to modernise the health service. Our argument is that, for sure, union members have not been given the opportunity to modernise the health service and that's what is needed. Not modernisation in the way that neo-liberals mean – cuts! – but modernisation in terms of change being led by front-line workers. It is the latter group of employees in the health service who are the best, not the only group, but the best, precisely because they are at the sharp end and can readily identify the problems and thus be instrumental in creating solutions together with patients. This is not happening and it is far away from anything proposed by Bengoa. Today, modernisation is synonymous with, and an understatement for, cuts. It sounds great, it's always great to talk about being modern: but in fact cutting services and jobs is not very modern at all. Unfortunately, NIPSA is far from being alone in embracing Bengoa's wonderful modernisation agenda.

UNISON's John Patrick Layton, speaking on BBC Radio Ulster *Talkback* (25 October 2016), praised the then Health Minister Michelle O'Neill and highlighted positives from his own perspective. He acknowledged that workers' terms and conditions would change, with "changes in employment, people moving here and there". He stressed that "engagement is crucial, engagement with the workforce". This is another way of "explaining" to the workforce they have to accept it. The unions are aware that front-line workers' terms and conditions are going to change. The reality for front-line workers, especially nurses and social workers, will be that they will be forced to assume more responsibility as they take on many of the tasks currently undertaken by GPs.

Unite the Union stressed that the restructuring process must be underpinned by adequate budgets and must guarantee equality of outcome for all patients. Unite Regional Officer Kevin McAdam said, "Unite the union has a positive outlook towards this process of reform. We will engage constructively in any processes which seek to achieve real efficiencies, improve services and value the contribution of all staff" (*ITV News*, 25 October 2016). However, it would be unusual if we were alone in being sceptical. For us, Bengoa has to be understood in the context of the agenda for full-scale privatisation of our health service. We can see the difficulties for the community presented by Bengoa's privatisation, top-down agenda if we take as an example just one area, that of addiction, where the community and front-line workers need to be in control. Part of the solution to the problems facing healthcare in Northern Ireland is to address the increasing addiction problem. A candidate was elected to public office to Derry City Council 2014 campaigning on the ground for the establishment of a detox unit. People in the community in Derry were calling for a much-needed service in response to the problem of addiction. There was no plan for innovative treatment or a detox unit to meet the needs of traumatised communities.

In our view, we require a public-owned health service operated by the people – the community and trade unions. Yet, rather than responding to public need, Bengoa's recommendations, as we highlighted above, drop the ball. Dr Tom Black, GP and British Medical Association (BMA) representative, supports the implementation of the Bengoa report, arguing the need for the engagement of what he describes as "not for profit Community interest companies" as the way forward.[20] In our view, the idea that we require companies to fund healthcare is the problem, not the solution. Bengoa will not sustain the post-war commitment to publicly funded healthcare at the point of delivery – and for the service overall in its full manifestation.

Elements of a plan identifying a number of key aspects of a social model would acknowledge the causes of life choices and their various coping mechanisms. Social models are holistic and empowering and they include evidenced-based treatments. They would of necessity include highly trained staff in psychological therapies and interventions. Our example drawn from just this one area, the provision of healthcare, and in terms of a specific issue, addiction, serves to make the point that for us – and one could identify a number of areas where trade unions and communities have common interests, common purpose – the problems we desperately need to address, in addition to having current and historical roots (see Chapter 6), require democratic and socially just responses. But our argument goes wider than this too for the point is that it is in this way, not by kowtowing to and extending the hand of "meanship" from management, that the real challenges to neo-liberalism can be established.

Bengoa is a whole lifeworld, a whole philosophy, away from the idea of a social plan for healthcare and this is why the trade unions should have been opposing it. They should be working to create a community- and worker-driven alternative to Stormont's neo-liberal marketisation agenda that has absolutely no conception of what a social plan for *socially created* health needs might look like. There is no plan to embrace a social model of health which attempts to address the broader influences of both current

20 Dr Black's 20 October 2016 address to the "committee for health" meeting is available in transcript form at http://aims. niassembly.gov.uk/officialreport/minutesofevidencereport. aspx?AgendaId=19411&eveID=10870

and historical health problems deriving from the long period of civil conflict (of a social, cultural, environmental and economic nature): it has to be more than just treating medical disorders as "simple" medical matters which can be described as disease and injury. What is required is a community trade union approach to prevent and tackle illnesses. It is a community and trade union approach, connecting social networks and social support that can best provide policies on health promotion.

Conclusion

We referred to the Right2Water campaign earlier in the chapter and clearly it would be unwise to draw exaggerated conclusions from this, but it does point to a much greater divergence of opinions and influences within the Irish trade union movement than has been the case for decades. Not everyone, in other words, supports the creeping privatisation. Yet – and although we should not need to be reminded of it, because it's an uncomfortable thought – the fact is that many in the labour movement, however mistaken they may be, see privatisation, if not as a good thing, then at least as a way to "preserve" what we have left. A strange way to think of preserving our public services by supporting, however lukewarm, an agenda that diminishes them. Strange but true. Yet, not everyone supports Bengoa's warm and insipidly embracing neo-liberal hegemony. There is diversity of course, not just in the north but throughout the island north and south, even though the response to the latter here in Northern Ireland might not feel like there is much of the time. There are reasons for opposition and diversity but it is reasonable to assume that the traumatic experience of the 2008 economic climate has caused otherwise passive trade unionists to take soundings from their membership and even from non-unionised workers.

Of course the pattern is different north and south but the driver of opposition is the outworking of neo-liberal failure, again albeit in somewhat different political economy terms, north and south of the border. It is this which has seen some movement in the development of a cross-border labour movement opposition, again, assuming various different forms, reflecting as it must, different patterns of opposition to neo-liberal domination.

Reflecting this trend is the emergence of trade union groups such as the Dublin-based Trade Union Left Forum (TULF).[21] Although clusters of articulate and highly motivated activists have always existed within the union movement, they've often struggled to have any impact at leadership level. However, in this case the TULF has been able to draw support from significant trade union personalities and this is indicative of a distinct change of mood music within organised labour in Ireland.

Although much of this progress has occurred in the Republic, many of the difficulties experienced in the southern jurisdiction are common to workers in the north. What is different, of course, are the well-known, long-standing and deep-running sectarian divisions. Consequently, it is important that the trade union movement in the six counties adopts a role supportive of the working class in general and one that sets it apart from the state and its functionaries. Moreover the movement of organised labour in Northern Ireland has to overcome the Peter Bunting policy of kowtowing to local and central government. By doing so the union movement can indeed overcome the sectarian curse by providing a strong class-based alternative (or genuine opposition) to the sterile and venal structure that is Stormont Mark II.

Northern Irish trade unionism needs to establish itself as a champion for working people and not just acting selfishly, with individual unions concentrating on representing

21   See http://www.tuleftforum.com/

only their own members' narrow work-related issues and ignoring all else. This strategy would mean trade unionists identifying issues that undermine the social wage while also campaigning to improve the standard of living for the working class universally.

Put in simple language, trade unions need to devise a strategy to combat austerity and neo-liberal economics. For example the case for ending the privatisation of areas of the NHS should be propagated and action organised to do so. We highlighted one way privatisation and marketisation might be challenged by examining the case of the Bengoa agenda for the so-called modernisation of key NHS services. We argued that what we might describe as "privatisation with a social-partnership face" has to be challenged not just by attacking private capital for what private capital will do – what else would anyone expect? One major difficulty has been, and continues to be, that the problem lies also within the labour movement. This is because some of our labour movement leaders imagine it is clever to be involved in what is in effect a dubious, and in any case superficial, partnership agenda, when what they are actually helping to deepen by their participation, is privatisation of our public services. There are choices to be made and the labour movement can respond in a proactive labour- and community-centred way, as the early opposition to Bunting's support for Fresh Start demonstrated. Even if this was initially only in statements, it nevertheless highlights the appetite for opposition to neo-liberalism more broadly within the labour movement.

Conclusion

It would be wrong to say there has been no progress at all since 1969. But 1969 came at the end of almost 50 years of neglect by the British state, where unionists were allowed to treat the Catholic community as unequal citizens. To my mind, since then, we went round in a very long, destructive circle to end up in a place close to where we started in 1924.

– Bernadette McAliskey (*Irish Times*, 22 September 2016)

Our argument throughout this book has been that the problems confronting people in Northern Ireland today, while in many respects not unlike those facing people across the world as a result of neo-liberal social and economic policies, have a particular dynamic resulting from the history of sectarian conflict. This sectarian conflict was fundamentally defined in and by a sectarian state which was changed as a result of the long insurgency that was brought to a close officially with the signing of the Good Friday Agreement in the spring of 1998.

The ways in which society in the north of Ireland/ Northern Ireland has sustained social and political divisions since the GFA is key to the current impasse. Specifically, the array of social and economic concerns in our communities, resulting from what we describe as neo-liberalism and neo-sectarianism, have created a deeply disempowering democratic deficit. In describing the current situation as one characterised as a democratic deficit, we wanted to go beyond the interesting notion that the 1998 GFA represented a "double transition" (to peace and neo-liberalism). While it could be argued that indeed something like a double transition has occurred, for us the notion of a double transition takes insufficient account of the interrelationship between the form taken by neo-liberalism in the north and the way in which it quite happily sits alongside sectarianism. More than this – neo-liberalism sustains it. This is a way of saying that the problem of neo-liberalism in Northern Ireland cannot be explained and challenged as if it is in some sense irrelevant to the particular way in which sectarianism has been reconstituted, and this is part of our beef with the dominant current within the official labour movement.

So, we've argued that while indeed much has changed, as the quote from Bernadette McAliskey makes clear, many problems remain that in their peculiar way derive from the persistence of sectarianism. Though this sectarianism is a product of long-term social divisions it has been, and continues to be, as the recent elections to the Assembly demonstrate, sustained by the dominant current within the political class in the north.

We would concur again with Bernadette McAliskey in her interview when she argued that "it's unacceptable from a socialist republican point of view that we are accommodating and facilitating sectarianism [allowing neo-liberalism to continue]".

Neo-liberalism for sure... Our two parties, despite their very different ideological and political starting points, have not only quite comfortably accommodated neo-liberalism, for the fact is they have extended it, made it work in a sectarian society. They have made sectarianism safe for neo-liberalism, made neo-liberalism safe for sectarianism. If you remain a passive supporter of the new status quo you may hope to avail of what little is available within your community, if you are tied to it. Reinforcing this structure of "encouraged passivity" is the fact that the social wage has been attacked so ferociously by the state – yes, the

British state, but the Stormont Assembly too. What is more, reducing the social wage (public services) has meant if you are not part of the system of acquiescence you will not benefit from the decreasing perks, never mind work, of the system. Further, what is worse is that rather than creating an environment of working-class opposition, encouraging a fightback against neo-liberal subordination, official labour and trade union organisations, for the most part, not all, but mostly, encourage apathy.

Our expectations in the north appear to be so low: you should remain apathetic as regards the bigger economic picture. And apathy so as not to undermine the peace process because otherwise you are a dissident. Dissent here in Northern Ireland has a special meaning as we know. In any other liberal democracy the idea doesn't exist in the way that it does in the north because it is assumed that liberal democracies are premised precisely upon the idea of difference, different voices ... different *dissenting* voices. Any attempt to challenge the status quo, whether it be political or economic here is immediately castigated as an "attack-on-the-peace-process" and if you do this you are a dissident. And everyone knows what that means – a dissident republican. If one doubts this we need only refer to the response by the NICTU and indeed by Bunting (above) to any organised labour movement rejection of support for Stormont's economic agenda most recently codified in Fresh Start. We will state that again: any response by the organised working class challenging Fresh Start, for which read, neo-liberal assault of the working class, is actually no more than an attack on the whole peace process. How have we come to this state of affairs in which an organised working-class struggle against capital is now put in the same space as those republicans who, in their very different ways, reject the peace process? That is to say, it conveniently ignores the fact that the term "dissident" is in any case a catch-all to frighten any and all republicans who criticise the peace process, as if those advocating armed struggle are the only republicans who reject it ... tarbrushing everyone.

Are you, or have you ever been, a critic of Fresh Start?

Many of us did not want to see the end of the Orange state just so that Catholics could now be on top. Again it's worth quoting Bernadette McAliskey from the interview above:

> If you see the problem purely in terms of unionism running the lives of nationalists, then you can say we have made significant progress. You can say, "Look, we now have Catholics at the very heart of power." But if that is not what you were ever about, then things may in fact be worse, because what we have is passive acquiescence in a society where the things I took for granted growing up have been destroyed.

We would concur with her too when she goes on to say that "[t]he economic and social brutality meted out to the Catholic, and Protestant, poor of the 1960s by a Unionist-dominated Stormont" is now given by neo-liberal social and economic policies. "Everything about this place reinforces sectarianism: segregated education, segregated living."

The central concern of our book has been to illustrate precisely the ways in which social and cultural segregation have reinvigorated sectarian divisions here. One kind of subordination has been replaced by another. Furthermore, in case anyone should imagine we are arguing that the sectarianism of the past is the same as the sectarianism of today's political reality, of the indispensable basis on which the Assembly operates, they would be very mistaken: as our quote from McAliskey and our book makes clear, it is good that being a Catholic does not form the basis of state repression. Now Catholic and Protestant workers alike can sleep under bridges and beg for bread... As McAliskey puts it, the GFA did not put the nail in the coffin of sectarianism per se. Yes Orange state sectarianism is over but the GFA is and has been concerned with "managing it and keeping it within the parameters of nonviolence and political control" (ibid.).

What now for this happy accommodation between neo-liberalism and sectarianism? And will the recent collapse and outcome of the Assembly elections in 2017 signal perhaps brighter days ahead? Wasn't the willingness of Sinn Féin to collapse the institutions of government a sign that moral courage, backbone, not to mention that thing so typically absent in a sectarian society, "normality", was for the first time taking the front seat in politics in the North? Or maybe it told us that in fact what was "normal" was the fact that indeed the economy, the North's neo-liberal economy, has been the big elephant in the room. The success of neo-liberalism, now that the state's hitherto publicly financed largess has been slashed, has depended decreasingly upon support for publicly financed social services and resources. To maintain the old (new!) alliance, the state has had to come up with new ways to feather-bed its variously sectarian hinterlands. Let us explore this further.

More than an energy crisis

The political crisis that brought down the Northern Ireland Assembly and Executive in early 2017 was the result not only of an ill-designed and poorly administered grant for renewable energy but was the inevitable product of a failing political entity. The fundamental problem facing the political parties in Northern Ireland is not how to go about restoring the institutions but what to do with a failed political entity locked helplessly within the United Kingdom.

This "cash for ash" scandal, as it was called, was the latest in a series of questionable projects and practices that go beyond merely undermining confidence in the North's ruling coalition. What the fiasco surrounding the renewable heating incentive (RHI) demonstrated was that the six-county state as currently structured is more an arrangement than an administration. As we have argued throughout, its survival now depends on a form of sectarian clientelism and economic opportunism, profoundly inimical to the well-being of working-class people.

In a society where conventional class politics have been ruthlessly curtailed through the cultivation of sectarian politics, there is a long history of rewarding important sections of the community from the public purse. Since the foundation of the northern state, government contracts were directed towards certain industries, construction projects were awarded to favoured companies, and certain farmers benefited disproportionately from exchequer largesse.

There was also a degree of subtlety to this that may surprise many outsiders. In the days before the civil rights movement, James Craig and his successors bought the Catholic hierarchy's acquiescence by granting them control of their congregation's education, a measure that simultaneously increased clerical influence through their power to award school-building contracts.

Since the GFA, this previously informal understanding has in effect been formalised into a designated structure that recognises and accommodates sectarianism rather than replacing it. As a consequence, political advantage accrues to those who are seen to provide best for their own supporters. This has led in turn to a series of squalid deals that have involved, among others, the dubious sale of NAMA property and the provision of a controversial £80 million social investment fund that is, in effect, controlled by the ruling DUP-Sinn Féin coalition as well as the now infamous RHI scheme.

Exacerbating this clearly unhealthy situation is the fact that under Assembly rules and procedures it is difficult to prevent unregulated practices happening and virtually impossible to punish those who cynically manipulate the flawed system. Under current legislation, any party commanding thirty votes (the DUP previously had thirty-eight) can issue what is known as a petition of concern, preventing any piece of legislation being enacted or criticism recorded. This device was used 115 times in the past five years and ensured that the DUP, in particular, was practically immune to censure.

Moreover, as the RHI scheme was designed to encourage business, industrial-scale farming and other non-domestic users to move from fossil fuels to renewable heating systems, we can be sure that poor pensioners, single mothers and just-about-managing families do not feature among the beneficiaries; and this fact takes us to the heart of the matter. This scheme was seen by several of the Stormont political parties as a means by which they could win favour with the small and medium business community and the larger farming sector. That they were doing so by what amounted to, at best, sharp practice was seen simply as the way the game is played here, through the judicious distribution of grace and favour.

The difficulty for the DUP and Sinn Féin, the two major parties, is that they are caught in a bind. Stormont as it is now constituted allows them to exert a certain amount of influence but grants no real power. The recent ruling by Britain's Supreme Court in relation to Article 50 (i.e. Brexit) made this painfully clear when it "unanimously ruled that devolved administrations did not need to be consulted and did not have a right to veto Article 50". It might well have added that deprived, as it is, of fiscal and political authority, this applies to all other matters of significance coming before the Assembly.

Making matters worse is the fact that those who have administered the North over the past ten years have no concrete plan for improving the situation. On the contrary, they have found themselves in the unenviable position of having to manage their responsibilities within parameters dictated by governments in London. How impoverished their response to this has been is evidenced by feeble initiatives such as the proposed reduction to corporation tax and appeals by the First and Deputy First Ministers to foreign transnationals to come and exploit the North's low-wage economy.

Moreover, it now appears that the absence of meaningful control over the economy may have played a significant part in the RHI (or "cash for ash") scandal. Approximately forty-five per cent of this grant aid was allocated to the poultry industry. An impartial observer could be forgiven for thinking that this was, in effect, a disguised subsidy for a low-tech industry that, unsupported, might easily have been undermined by competition from abroad.

The North of Ireland once had an extensive and profitable industrial economy, most notably in shipbuilding, rope manufacture and textiles. Now however, most of this has been replaced by services, some in the civil service but many are of the low-paid and precarious call centre type. As a consequence, the six-county economy does not produce the scale of private-sector profit that it once did. No longer, therefore, is the region home to the self-contained wealth-earning merchant and manufacturing class that once governed the area.

Northern Ireland has the lowest gross disposable household income (GDHI) in the United Kingdom and has few prospects of improving on this sorry statistic.[22] One result of this is what might be described as economic

22 For more details see "Regional Gross Disposable Household Income (GDHI): 1997 to 2014" on the Office for National Statistics website at https://www.ons.gov.uk/economy/regionalaccounts/grossdisposablehouseholdincome/bulletins/regionalgrossdisposablehouseholdincomegdhi/2014#main-points

opportunism, manifesting itself on occasions as organised fraud, clientelism and the type of dubious or questionable practices such as those connected to the RHI scandal.

Whatever conclusion will eventually be drawn from enquiries into the RHI affair, it exposes inherent weaknesses in Stormont's political and economic structures. The northern political entity is a peripheral region of the United Kingdom locked into London's political and economic orbit. Unable to chart its own course, Northern Ireland is reduced to operating an opportunistic economic policy regulated and contaminated through the mean practising of sectarian politics. Therefore, while the Assembly and the Executive may eventually be restored, they will continue to huff and puff and do little to improve the dismal lot of the region's working class.

As with so many other states failed by a colonial past and contemporary capitalism, the North needs a transformative strategy. This requires frankness, honesty and a willingness to contemplate options that will not please everyone. The northern state, as currently constituted, is a failure and has to be replaced. That change will come about is no longer in doubt. The fallout from Brexit, Scottish disenchantment with London, and changing demographics are among the factors that guarantee this. As if these were the only considerations! As we write our conclusions we can add to the mix the outcome of elections to the Northern Ireland Assembly, brought down as a result of the scandal attending the RHI affair.

Whatever else can be said of the results, of which there is surely plenty, they have delivered a defining blow to old-style Unionism. For the first time since the northern state was set up in 1921, mainstream political Unionism does not command an overall majority either in seats or within the electorate. This has to be qualified, however, by pointing to the fact that within the six-county state there remains a majority in favour of maintaining the union with Great Britain.

This apparent contradiction is explained by the fact that while the two largest non-Unionist parties, Sinn Fein and the SDLP, have achieved a rough symmetry with the two largest pro-Union parties, the DUP and the UUP, there is a middle position occupied by the Alliance Party. Largely middle class and economically conservative, the Alliance Party is broadly speaking in favour of the Union but significantly not in the fashion practised for decades. Old-style Unionism brashly asserts that the Union must be maintained at all costs, remains in denial that change is either possible or negotiable, and believes it has a divine right to govern the North.

A brief overview of the election statistics illustrates the extent of the political shift that has arisen from structural changes in the area. Parties clearly defining themselves primarily as Unionist of the old school received less than forty-five per cent of the vote and gained forty seats. Three parties that are clearly not Unionist received just less than forty-two per cent of the vote and gained forty seats. Two parties that may be described as Unionist with a small "u" received over eleven per cent of the vote and took the remaining ten seats.

For almost a century, Unionism was able to maintain its intransigent position in the six counties through a combination of factors. In the early decades of the twentieth century Britain's ruling class saw Ireland as a strategically important area and therefore actively encouraged the partition of Ireland with the creation of the Unionist mini-state that was and is Northern Ireland. The carefully selected boundaries of this new state ensured a demographic make-up that allowed for a permanent Unionist majority. Furthermore, prior to globalisation, Northern Ireland had a profitable industrial base that created an indigenous bourgeoisie that owed its wealth in large part to the British Empire.

The north of Ireland is today of much less strategic or economic interest to Britain and the demographic make-up is heading inexorably towards a Nationalist or republican majority. Moreover, the region's economy is at best flatlining although in truth the area is in gradual economic decline.

Due to the long-established practice of viewing northern Irish politics as fundamentally a binary contest between pro- and anti-Union positions, commentary on the recent election has naturally focused on whether Sinn Fein may or may not demand a border poll. Current observations strongly indicate that a referendum now would return a majority in favour of the Union, causing some Unionists (such as John Taylor) to claim that the impact on Unionism of the election setback is more psychological than a fundamental threat to its position.

There exists, however, a more nuanced interpretation of what has occurred. While the constitutional position of Northern Ireland remains intact – for the time being at least – there is now a working majority in favour of what may be described as the politics of accommodation. If for example, majority rule were to be restored, any possible administration would have to involve a coalition including the politically ambivalent Alliance and Green parties. There is not, at present, any prospect of a return to Stormont majoritarianism. Not only would it be in contravention of the GFA but it sits uneasily with non-Unionists since for years, majority rule was merely a euphemism for Unionist absolutism.

Nevertheless, these changes are significant, albeit coming with some caveats. Most important it has to be recognised that while evidence of a more accommodating constituency exists within Unionism, there remains quite a large hard-line majority. In order to address this reality it is important that a twin-track approach is adopted in the coming years. On one hand it is crucial that the reality of change is identified, highlighted and spoken of. On the other hand, concrete action has to be taken to demonstrate, especially to the pro-Unionist working class, that such change can and will support them in their struggles against neo-liberal globalisation.

Simply waiting for events to take their course, however, is not an option in the volatile political arena that is Northern Ireland. The only responsible approach is to ensure change happens under the best possible conditions and with maximum support from within the working class. To do so it will be necessary to introduce a programme that demonstrates (even if it cannot be immediately implemented) a clear and reasonable path towards a new and better society. Core issues impacting detrimentally on working-class communities have to be highlighted and solutions identified over the short, medium and long term. A notable one which we've identified above includes better health provision recognising especially, right at the start, the fact that the North, as a so-called post-conflict society, requires special measures to respond to those numerous people and their communities affected by the long civil conflict.

What's more, it does not take long to list other critical areas that would form the basis of a transformative programme. Just as in the Republic, there is a homeless/rental housing crisis in the North that can only be addressed by a comprehensive public housing strategy. The continuing privatisation of the NHS has to be halted and rolled back and this means engaging with trade union leaderships in their various guises. Workers' rights need (re)defining, asserting and defending. Financially secure and generous care for the aged must be made a priority so that it is seen as a fundamental right for all of us who might be lucky enough to grow old. And the greatest stain of all – ubiquitous food banks in twenty-first-century Northern Ireland – must be addressed and the need for them ended for all time.

In order to implement such a strategy it will be necessary to build a movement around progressive forces and identify a means to engage with people across sectarian divisions irrespective of gender or ethnicity. Let's be honest, this won't be easy but the alternative is to do nothing while tolerating existing failure, as we wait for the situation to inevitably get worse. For the sake of the long-suffering working people of the area, it's surely time to begin thinking of a viable alternative to what is now in place in Stormont.

Postscript
The Assembly Collapses 2017:
The Final Curtain?

A constant theme running through this book has been that the six-county political entity of Northern Ireland is a failed state. The events that have taken place since the collapse of the Stormont Executive and Assembly in January 2017 have done little to challenge that assessment.[23] This judgement is based on the fact that those in favour of maintaining Northern Ireland as an integral part of the kingdom appear to be unable to make the type of concessions necessary for the current status quo to remain into the future.

As has been referred to elsewhere in this book, the Northern Irish state had its origins in a colonialism that evolved into imperialism. The seventeenth-century colonial population that ruled over the northern part of Ireland and shared the region with its earlier inhabitants, later became virtually an imperial garrison as the British Empire extended (and was challenged) through the nineteenth and twentieth centuries. The fifty years of

23 Quoted from "How Dumb Are the DUP? How Deep Is the Ocean?", posted on *The Broken Elbow* on 14 February 2018:

When a revolutionary group, dedicated to the use of violence to overturn the constitutional status quo, which kept its violence going for over three decades to achieve that goal, killing hundreds of people, maiming thousands more and causing countless millions in damage, then decides a) to call a ceasefire while its leaders don smart suits, grooms and styles their hair and bleaches their teeth, b) allows its weapons to be destroyed and winds down the bulk of its military strength

absolute power enjoyed by this community following the establishment of the state in 1921 did nothing to change their view that they had an almost divine right to rule, a mindset that has proven extremely difficult to change in the intervening years.

When pressurised at the end of the 1990s to accept political change, they did so under duress, with bad grace and with little desire either to accommodate their erstwhile opponents or mend relationships fractured over decades if not centuries. Crucially, the Unionist leadership either failed to recognise or chose to ignore the existing sociopolitical and economic reality of the situation in which they and their supporters now find themselves.

The balance of political forces in the world in relation to the United Kingdom has changed greatly since those post-WWI days of the 1920s when the Northern Irish state was formed. Britain no longer has an empire nor does it view Northern Ireland as essential to its strategic defensive requirements. Globalisation has robbed the Northern Irish economy of its once powerful manufacturing base and thus deprives it of possible financial autonomy. Moreover, the demographic make-up of the area is changing with its non-Unionist population growing inexorably, raising the distinct possibility of a non-Unionist majority sometime in the next twenty-five years.

---

and c) takes seats in a parliament it once swore to burn to the ground and then substitutes a cultural demand for a political one – in this case for the right to use the language of its ancestors on street signs and the like – then the reaction of its erstwhile enemy should be:

i) Throw hats in the air with joy;
ii) Invite their former enemies to a slap-up dinner;
iii) Scowl with anger and retreat into the bunkers?

Answers on a postcard to Arlene Foster, Dumbest Political Leader In Europe, Last Chance Saloon, End Of The Line Avenue, Stormont Buildings, Belfast.

Rather than face the challenge presented by changing circumstances, the largest Unionist party, the DUP, seems to have set itself the task of frustrating as many initiatives sponsored by Sinn Féin as possible and in the process alienating that section of the community represented by the republican party. From the restoration of the institutions of Stormont in 2008, the DUP appeared determined to demonstrate that its *raison d'être* was more to foil Sinn Fein than to provide even-handed governance for the area. And this in spite of the fact that the two parties were sharing the administration.

DUP obstruction included preventing attempts to introduce legislation in support of the Irish language, a point-blank refusal to endorse an interpretative centre promoting peace and reconciliation on the old Long Kesh prison site, foot-dragging on the development of a much-needed motorway from Derry to Dublin, and blocking funding to review legacy cases involving state forces.

Compounding the seemingly endless negativity from the DUP was a cavalier attitude towards transparency and accountability. The party used the Petition of Concern device to stall legislation and or censure motions on eighty-six occasions between 2011 and 2015, almost three times as many as laid down by either Sinn Fein or the SDLP (*The Detail*, 29 September 2016). Incredibly, Sinn Féin long remained unwilling to collapse the Assembly government institutions in spite of what can be described as ongoing provocative behaviour from the DUP.

In 2015, for example, DUP stalwart Nelson McCausland was accused of putting party before public interest by an Assembly committee of inquiry. The inquiry found that McCausland had acted inappropriately when he attempted to extend maintenance firm Red Sky's multimillion-pound contract with the Northern Ireland Housing Executive in spite of the company's many faults, the least of which were overcharging (*The Detail*, 12 September 2012). Nothing was done to sanction the minister responsible for this questionable behaviour.

There was also a disturbing reluctance to deal with issues arising from the NAMA funding scandal although the suspicion has lingered for so long that senior DUP party personnel had questions to answer (*BBC News*, 24 September 2015). Again, it seemed that the entire issue was brushed quietly aside.

In the aftermath of the British referendum to decide whether the UK would remain in or leave the European Union, it was discovered that the DUP had accepted almost £500,000 from a mysterious source. This money was used to fund an expensive, pro-leave, advertising campaign in London in spite of the fact the DUP only ever stands candidates in Northern Ireland (*Open Democracy*, 28 February 2017). Once more the hard-line Unionist party brushed aside all queries and criticism and continued as if nothing had happened.

Ultimately, it was the DUP leadership's refusal to deal expeditiously and transparently with the Renewable Heat Incentive (RHI) fiasco which proved to be the final straw that precipitated the collapse of the Assembly in January 2017. How this came about is revealing. The RHI scheme was ostensibly an energy initiative set up to encourage businesses and domestic users to switch from fossil fuels to renewable sources. A major flaw in its set-up and implementation meant it went vastly over budget, with scheme participants getting more in grant aid than the cost of their inputs. The issue was highlighted in late 2016 by a BBC investigative programme, which also revealed that some grantees had actually criminally abused the scheme. Some had cheated by heating vacant premises in order to claim large payouts while others had manipulated their burners in order to record inflated readings.

Oddly, Sinn Fein was at first reluctant to provoke a crisis by demanding the resignation of the minister in charge of the department with responsibility for the programme at the time of its original roll-out and development, the by-then First Minister Arlene Foster. This was in spite of a dramatic television interview with Jonathan Bell, Mrs Foster's party colleague and successor at the Department of Enterprise, Trade and Investment. Speaking to the BBC's Stephen Nolan, Bell appeared to lay blame for the RHI debacle at the feet of Mrs Foster and her advisers.

These serious allegations notwithstanding, Sinn Féin did not demand a resignation but merely asked the First Minister to step aside temporarily until an interim report would be issued. A precedent had been set for this procedure a few years earlier by Foster's predecessor Peter Robinson when his wife had been accused of abusing her position as an elected representative to gain advantage for a close acquaintance.

Notwithstanding the fact that Sinn Féin was well within its rights to demand decisive action from the First Minister, Mrs Foster dismissed the party's request to make any gesture that would indicate a recognition that ministerial responsibility meant anything to a member of the DUP. As the issue generated enormous interest in the print and broadcast media, it appeared that the Unionist party was simply going to sit out the storm as they had in the past. Everything changed dramatically when the DUP's Communities Minister Paul Givan used a dismissive tweet to cancel a modest £50,000 grant for the Irish-language community. For a Minister that had reinstated a £200,000 grant for Orange marching bands six months earlier, this action was taken to be gratuitously offensive to the Nationalist community at a sensitive time.

With this, the patience and tolerance of Sinn Féin's activists were finally exhausted. At a stormy meeting in a Belfast community centre, rank-and-file members of the party demanded that its leadership withdraw from the Executive. Recognising the impossibility of continuing without grass-root support, the party's Deputy First Minister Martin McGuinness resigned, bringing down the executive and precipitated elections to a new assembly in March 2017.

The March elections proved to be a traumatic experience for Unionism. The number of members to be elected to the new assembly had been reduced from 108 to ninety and it was thus inevitable that some MLAs would fail to be re-elected. Nevertheless, Unionism did not expect to find that it would lose its overall majority in a Northern Irish Parliament for the first time in the history of the northern state.

Forty seats went to the two pro-Unionist parties, while a similar number of seats were claimed by anti-partition parties. The remaining ten seats were divided between the Alliance and Green parties, which describe themselves as neutral on the constitutional issue in spite of drawing their support from pro-Union communities. The DUP remained the largest single party but only by one seat: twenty-eight in comparison to twenty-seven for Sinn Féin.

Two aspects of the election had a deep psychological and practical impact on the Unionist world view. On one hand, a bitterly contested election had not been able to prevent a significant number of pro-Union people withdrawing support from Unionist parties. On the other hand, the electoral map starkly illustrated the outcome with Sinn Féin's support base creating a crescent-shaped encirclement of the Unionist heartland (please refer to the photo insert inside this book for an illustration).

While the constitutional position of Northern Ireland within the UK was not immediately threatened by the election result, there was now a working majority in favour of what may be described as the politics of accommodation.

Moreover, the narrow margin separating the two main political blocks encouraged Sinn Féin to repeat its call for a referendum to decide whether to retain the northern state or to seek unity with the Republic of Ireland. While this had been a constant factor in Unionist calculations for decades, the possibility of undermining the status of Northern Ireland as a part of the UK had for decades appeared a remote concept. This was no longer quite so obvious. Writing in the Unionist-supporting *News Letter* a few days after the Assembly elections, deputy editor Ben Lowry said, "If the correlation between Catholicism and Irish nationalism remains similarly high in the decades to come, Unionism is in deep trouble given the small but relentless demographic change" (4 March 2017).

Under the circumstances, it would appear that the rational option for Unionism would have been to take steps to negotiate an agreed future before discovering they had lost their bargaining power. However this was not to be and three months later, finding that they held the balance of power in the House of Commons following Theresa May's disastrous general election, the DUP agreed to support a Conservative Party government. While granting the party some temporary advantage, it did little to improve its standing relationship with the non-Unionist community in Northern Ireland or indeed, with the British Labour Party.

Meanwhile, Sinn Féin was no longer concentrating solely on Northern Ireland since it had a major involvement in electoral politics in the Republic of Ireland. With a realistic possibility of participating in a coalition government in Dublin, the party was in no rush to find an accommodation in the North. When it did agree to re-enter talks in Belfast in early 2018, it did so with a much greater degree of flexibility than might have been expected, but Unionism was unable to grasp the opportunity.

According to the usually well-informed Denis Bradley, writing in the *Irish Times*, Sinn Féin had agreed that Arlene Foster would remain as First Minister, that there would be no agreement to liberalise legislation on civic marriage or abortion, and that the Petition of Concern would remain virtually unchanged (*Irish Times*,

21 February 2018). Going by this as yet unchallenged assessment, it would appear that the DUP was emerging practically unscathed from the RHI scandal. After all, RHI was a costly fiasco of the DUP's own making, about which even Baroness Paisley said that Mrs Foster should have stood aside.

Having secured what promised to be a favourable outcome under difficult circumstances, it was obvious that some reasonable ground would have had to be conceded across the table. In this case a modest demand in relation to cultural recognition. Without the minimal concession of an Irish language act, Mary Lou McDonald and Michelle O'Neill would have left the negotiations empty-handed and unable to sell the deal to their rank and file. Unionist negotiators undoubtedly were aware of this, yet chose to collapse the talks rather than risk alienating reactionary sections of their electorate.

In light of the circumstances outlined above, it is clear that Northern Ireland cannot indefinitely remain a country in aspic. It is difficult, therefore, to see how Unionism can survive in the long term, suffering as it does from an inability to change or compromise even in its own self-interest. The question now is how change will be effected in the future. The region's recent bloody history doesn't give enormous scope for optimism.

Yet there are some signs that things may not be as foreboding as they appear. A recent letter to the *Belfast Telegraph* from 105 civic Unionists offered to discuss the future of Northern Ireland in a reasoned and rational debate (26 February 2018). They ended their letter by stating,

> We wish to unite, not divide, and in encouraging transparency we call upon civic nationalism and others to engage with us in frank and fulsome debates about the many values and beliefs that are commonly shared and are vital to transforming the issues that we face.

These sentiments pose two distinct challenges, one for Irish republicans and something different for Unionists. For republicans, the challenge is not just to respond to an invitation to discuss the future but to offer something concrete and attractive that rises above nationalism. The task for Unionism may be more straightforward but much more difficult. Unionism has to find sufficient support to make the above-mentioned invitation more than the desire of an insignificant minority within its constituency.

The future of Northern Ireland is not decided just yet.

Bibliography

agendaNi (18 October 2016) "Politics with a Small 'P'". n.a. http://www.agendani.com/politics-small-p/

Anheier, H.K. (2002) *The Third Sector in Europe: Five Theses*. Civil Society Working Paper 12. http://eprints. lse.ac.uk/29051/1/CSWP12.pdf

Azevedo, F., and Haase, D. (November 2017) *Northern Ireland PEACE Programme*. http://www.europarl.europa. eu/ftu/pdf/en/FTU_3.1.9.pdf

BBC News (28 June 2000) "Threatened Hospital Campaign Continues". n.a. (http://news.bbc.co.uk/2/hi/ uk_news/northern_ireland/809408.stm)

BBC News (31 July 2000) "Campaigners Lose Hospital Battle". n.a. http://news.bbc.co.uk/1/hi/northern_ ireland/858753.stm

BBC News (26 November 2014) "Spotlight: Research Services Ireland Got £700,000 in Sinn Féin Expenses". n.a. http://www.bbc.co.uk/news/ uk-northern-ireland-30204080

BBC News (24 September 2015) "Nama NI Deal: The Key Figures and the Background You Need to Know". n.a. http://www.bbc.co.uk/news/ uk-northern-ireland-33462375

BBC News (29 October 2015) "Féile an Phobail: Concerns Over £550,000 Public Funding Given to Festival". By Robbie Meredith. http://www.bbc.co.uk/news/uk-northern-ireland-34671850

BBC News (4 February 2016) "Suicide: Northern Ireland has UK's Highest Rate for Second Year in a Row". n.a. http://www.bbc.com/news/uk-northern-ireland-35491402

Belfast Telegraph (7 April 2014) "The Young: Two Thirds of Our Young People Want to Build Their Future Outside Northern Ireland". By Liam Clarke. https://www.belfasttelegraph.co.uk/news/northern-ireland/the-young-two-thirds-of-our-young-people-want-to-build-their-future-outside-northern-ireland-30159933.html

Belfast Telegraph (16 June 2014) "Northern Irish Workers: Huge Wage Divide Compared to UK Peers Doing Same Job". By Claire McNeilly. https://www.belfasttelegraph.co.uk/news/northern-ireland/northern-irish-workers-huge-wage-divide-compared-to-uk-peers-doing-same-job-30356587.html

Belfast Telegraph (11 November 2015) "Civil Servant Richard Pengelly Criticised Over 'Vague' Answers at Nama Inquiry". n.a. https://www.belfasttelegraph.co.uk/news/northern-ireland/civil-servant-richard-pengelly-criticised-over-vague-answers-at-nama-inquiry-34191087.html

Belfast Telegraph (12 November 2015) "Stagnant Northern Ireland Economy Raises Fears for Long-term Unemployed". By Margaret Canning. https://www.belfasttelegraph.co.uk/business/news/stagnant-northern-ireland-economy-raises-fears-for-longterm-unemployed-34192748.html

Belfast Telegraph (30 December 2015) "Northern Ireland Wages Fall 5% in Seven Years as UK Average Pay Suffers Double-Digit Dip". John Mulgrew. https://www.belfasttelegraph.co.uk/business/news/northern-ireland-wages-fall-5-in-seven-years-as-uk-average-pay-suffers-doubledigit-dip-34322438.html

Belfast Telegraph (29 January 2016) "Northern Irish Growth to Remain Slower than the Rest of the UK, Warns PwC". By Margaret Canning. https://www.belfasttelegraph.co.uk/business/news/northern-ireland-growth-to-remain-slower-than-rest-of-the-uk-warns-pwc-34405331.html

Belfast Telegraph (29 January 2016) "Farming Incomes Plummet by 40% in Northern Ireland". By Adrian Rutherford. https://www.belfasttelegraph.co.uk/news/northern-ireland/farming-incomes-plummet-by-40-in-northern-ireland-34405918.html

Belfast Telegraph (15 April 2016) "Record Numbers Relying on Food Banks Across Northern Ireland". By Allan Preston. https://www.belfasttelegraph.co.uk/news/northern-ireland/record-numbers-relying-on-food-banks-across-northern-ireland-34628832.html

Belfast Telegraph. (8 November 2016) "24% of Children in Northern Ireland 'Living in Poverty'". n.a. https://www.belfasttelegraph.co.uk/news/northern-ireland/24-of-children-in-northern-ireland-living-in-poverty-35196811.html

Belfast Telegraph (12 November 2016) "Executive 'Must Do More to Tackle Unacceptable Rise in Homelessness'". By Cate McCurry. https://www.belfasttelegraph.co.uk/news/northern-ireland/executive-must-do-more-to-tackle-unacceptable-rise-in-homelessness-35208622.html

Belfast Telegraph (26 February 2018) "Who Are the 105 'Civic Unionists' Backing Call for Inclusive Debate on Rights and Equality?" n.a. https://www.belfasttelegraph.co.uk/news/northern-ireland/who-are-the-105-civic-unionists-backing-call-for-inclusive-debate-on-rights-and-equality-36646164.html

Bell, G. (1979) *The Protestants of Ulster,* London: Pluto Press.

Bengoa, R. (25 September 2013) "Transforming Health Care: An Approach to System-Wide Implementation". *International Journal of Integrated Care.* Jul-Sep: e039. https://www.ncbi.nlm.nih.gov/pmc/articles/PMC3812354/

Berger, J., and Mohr, J. (1975) *A Seventh Man: Migrant Workers in Europe.* London: Penguin Books.

Bew, P., Gibbon, P., and Patterson, H. (2002) *Northern Ireland: 1921/2001 Political Forces and Social Classes.* London: Serif.

European Commission (2014) *Northern Ireland in Europe: Report of the European Commission's Northern Ireland Task Force 2017–2014*. http://ec.europa.eu/regional_ policy/sources/activity/ireland/report2014.pdf

Farrell, M. (1976) *Northern Ireland the Orange State*. London: Pluto Press.

Financial Times (23 May 2014) "A City in a World of its Own". By Gillian Tett. (Web address unavailable)

Financial Times (3 December 2015) "UK Public Services: Reshaping the State". By Sarah Neville. https://www. ft.com/content/5217cc44-92de-11e5-bd82-c1fb87bef7af

Garvey, B., and Stewart, P. (2015) "Migrant Workers and the North of Ireland: Between Neo-Liberalism and Sectarianism". *Work, Employment and Society*, doi: 10.1177/0950017014556800 March 6

Garvey, B., Stewart, P., Kulinska, J., and Campuzano, R. (2010) *The New Workers* [Film]. Belfast: Creative Workers Co-operative.

Guardian (22 January 2013) "Charities' Silence on Government Policy is Tantamount to Collusion". By Zoe Williams. https://www. theguardian.com/commentisfree/2013/jan/22/ charities-silence-government-policy

Harvey, D. (2010) *The Enigma of Capital and the Crises of Capitalism*. London: Profile Books.

Holgate, J., Pollert, A., Keles, J., and Kumarappan, L. (2012) "Union Decline and Voice Among Minority Ethnic Workers; Do Community Support Networks Help Fill the Gap?" *Urban Studies* 49(3): 491-508.

Irish News (26 September 2014) "British and Unionists Won 'War' Says Troubles Journalist Peter Taylor". By Marie Louise McConville. http://www.irishnews.com/news/2014/09/26/news/british-and-unionists-won-war-says-troubles-journalist-peter-taylor-103125/

Irish News (14 August 2015) "Casement Park: Sports Minister Denies 'Grubby Scheme'". By Brendan Hughes. http://www.irishnews.com/news/2015/08/14/news/casement-park-sports-minister-denies-grubby-scheme--227194/

Irish News (9 November 2015) "Linda Ervine: I Realised Irish Belonged to Me – a Protestant – and I Fell in Love With It." By Linda Ervine. http://www.irishnews.com/news/northernirelandnews/2015/11/09/news/linda-ervine-i-gained-so-much-from-learning-the-irish-language-318630/

Irish News (19 November 2015) "Money for Shared School Campus Drive to be Reallocated." By Simon Doyle. http://www.irishnews.com/news/2015/11/19/news/money-for-shared-school-campus-drive-to-be-reallocated-327450/

Irish News (16 December 2015) "ICTU Opts for Pragmatism Over Stormont Fresh Start Protest". By John Manley. http://www.irishnews.com/news/2015/12/16/news/ictu-opts-for-pragmatism-over-protest-355099/

Irish News (5 February 2016) "Trade Union Group Faces Criticism Over Support for Fresh Start". By Connla Young. http://www.irishnews.com/news/2016/02/05/news/trade-union-group-faces-criticism-over-support-for-fresh-start-406842/

Irish News (15 February 2016) "GP Tells of Losing Patients to Heroin for First Time". By Seanín Graham. http://www.irishnews.com/news/2016/02/15/news/gp-tells-of-losing-patients-to-heroin-for-first-time-417607/

Irish News (30 September 2016) "UDA Linked Group to Manage £1.7 million Investment for East Belfast". By Allison Morris. http://www.irishnews.com/news/northernirelandnews/2016/09/30/news/uda-linked-group-to-manage-1-7-million-investment--714427/

Irish News (23 November 2016) "Stormont Probe Over Minister Claiming Rent for Office Owned by MLA's Husband". By Brenda Hughes. http://www.irishnews.com/paywall/tsb/irishnews/irishnews/irishnews//news/northernirelandnews/2016/11/23/news/stormont-probe-over-minister-claiming-rent-for-office-owned-by-mla-s-husband-796561/content.html

Irish Times (8 July 2015) "Ictu Back Policy that Rejects Imposition of Water Charges". n.a. https://www.irishtimes.com/business/work/ictu-back-policy-that-rejects-imposition-of-water-charges-1.2278067

Irish Times (28 October 2015) "Emma Pengelly Fast-Tracked as DUP Junior Minister". By Gerry Moriarty. https://www.irishtimes.com/news/ireland/irish-news/emma-pengelly-fast-tracked-as-dup-junior-minister-1.2408726

Irish Times (22 September 2016) "Bernadette McAliskey: 'I Am Astounded I Survived. I Made Mad Decisions'". By Kitty Holland. https://www.irishtimes.com/life-and-style/people/bernadette-mcaliskey-i-am-astounded-i-survived-i-made-mad-decisions-1.2798293

Irish Times (21 February 2018) "Denis Bradley: How Do You Solve a Problem Like Unionism?" By Denis Bradley. https://www.irishtimes.com/opinion/denis-bradley-how-do-you-solve-a-problem-like-unionism-1.3398989

ITV News (25 October 2016) "Unions React to Bengoa Report into Health Care". n.a. http://www.itv.com/news/utv/2016-10-25/unions-react-to-bengoa-report-into-health-care/

Jack, I. (24 September 2016). "Without Oil Money, the Nationalist Dream Will Have to Run on Emotion." *The Guardian.* https://www.theguardian.com/commentisfree/2016/sep/24/scotland-oil-money-nationalist-dream-nicola-sturgeon-independence

Jamieson, R., Shirlow, P., and Grounds, A. (2010) *Ageing and Social Exclusion Among Former Politically Motivated Prisoners in Northern Ireland.* Belfast: Changing Ageing Partnership.

Jarman, N. (2004) "From War to Peace? Changing Patterns of Violence in Northern Ireland 1990-2003". *Terrorism and Political Violence* 16(3): 420-38.

Jarman, N. (2006) Diversity, Economy and Policy: New Patterns of Migration to Northern Ireland". *Shared Space* 2: 45-62.

Jarman, N., and Lucas, O. (2016) *Poverty and Ethnicity: Key Messages for Northern Ireland.* Joseph Rowntree Foundation.

Kelly, B. (2012) "Neoliberal Belfast: Disaster Ahead?" *Irish Marxist Review* 1(2), Summer.

Kelly, G. (2012) *Progressing Good Relations and Reconciliation in Post-Agreement Northern Ireland.* University of Ulster: INCORE.

Mac Flynn, P. (18 July 2014) *Hours and Earnings in the Northern Ireland Labour Market.* Nevin Economic Research Institute (NERI) Working Paper (WP) Series 2014/No 17. https://www.nerinstitute.net/download/pdf/hours_and_earnings_in_ni_neri_wp17.pdf

MacIntyre-Kemp, G. (2 September 2016) "Gordon MacIntyre-Kemp: Brown Can Say Whatever He Likes. His Time Is Gone." *The National.* http://www.thenational.scot/news/14870433.Gordon_MacIntyre_Kemp__Brown_can_say_whatever_he_likes__His_time_is_gone/

Maguire, M. (1988) "Work, Locality and Social Control". *Work, Employment and Society* 12(1): 71-87.

McAliskey, B., Yam, P., O'Neill, M., Godfrey, A., and O'Neill, B. (2006) *Black and Minority Ethnic Access to Services in the Southern Health and Social Services Board Area,* Dungannon: STEP/WahHep/SHSSB/Southern Area Children's Planning Committee, 3, 7, 45, 50, 52.

McAuley, J.W. (2015) *Very British Rebels? The Culture and Politics of Ulster Loyalism.* London: Bloomsbury Publishing.

McCabe, C. (2013) *The Double Transition: The Economic and Political Transition of Peace*. Belfast: Irish Congress of Trade Unions.

McCaffrey, R. (5 September 2013) *The Civic Forum*. Research paper.

McGovern, J., Meas, W.H., and Webb, M.A. (2011) *Supporting refugee and Asylum Seeking Families Living in Northern Ireland*. Belfast: Barnardo's Northern Ireland.

McKearney, T. (2011) *The Provisional IRA, from Insurrection to Parliament*. London: Pluto Books.

McKeever, G., and O'Rawe, M. (2007) "Political Ex-prisoners and Policing in Transitional Societies Testing the Boundaries of New Conceptions of Citizenship and Security". *International Journal of Law in Context* 3(2): 105-25.

McLaughlin, G., and Baker, S. (2015) *The British Media and Bloody Sunday*. Bristol: Intellect.

McVeigh, R. (2007) *Migrant Workers and Their Families in Northern Ireland: A Trade Union Response*. Belfast: Irish Congress of Trade Unions.

McVeigh, S. (2012) "Sinn Fein in Government". *Irish Marxist Review* 1(1). http://www.irishmarxistreview.net/index.php/imr/article/view/7/7

Moloney, E. (14 February 2018) "How Dumb Are the DUP? How Deep Is the Ocean?" *The Broken Elbow*. https://thebrokenelbow.com/2018/02/14/how-dumb-are-the-dup-how-deep-is-the-ocean/

News Letter (21 April 2014) "Why Not Voting Might Be the Only Way to Change Things". By Alex Kane. https://www.newsletter.co.uk/news/opinion/why-not-voting-might-be-the-only-way-to-change-things-1-6012570

News Letter (7 June 2016) "SF Minister: I Will Use Private Health Firms to Clear Backlog". By Sam McBride. https://www.newsletter.co.uk/news/sf-minister-i-will-use-private-health-firms-to-clear-backlog-1-7418328

News Letter (4 March 2017) "Ben Lowry: Northern Ireland's Future in the UK Now Depends on Alliance Voters". By Ben Lowry. https://www.newsletter.co.uk/news/opinion/ben-lowry-northern-ireland-s-future-in-the-uk-now-depends-on-alliance-voters-1-7850546

Northern Ireland Association for the Care and Resettlement of Offenders (NIACRO) (2008) Position paper.

Northern Ireland Council for Ethnic Minorities (NICEM) (2013) *Race and Criminal Justice in Northern Ireland*. http://nicem.org.uk/uploads/publications/Race_and_Criminal_Justice_2013.pdf (Accessed January 2013; no longer available)

Northern Ireland Council for Voluntary Action (NICVA) (2009) "Workforce". *State of the Sector V*, 60-69 http://www.nicva.org/sites/default/files/d7content/attachments-resources/sosv-workforce.pdf

O'Dowd, L., Rolston, B., and Tomlinson, M. (1980) *Northern Ireland: Between Civil Rights and Civil War*. London: CSE Books.

Office of National Statistics (ONS) (30 April 2014),
*Analysis of Employee Contracts that do not Guarantee
a Minimum Number of Hours.* www.ons.gov.uk/ons/
dcp171776_361578.pdf

Office of National Statistics (ONS) and Department
of Enterprise, Trade and Investment (DETI) (2009)
Labour Force Survey. Newport: ONS, 22-44.

Ong, A. (1999) *Flexible Citizenship: The Cultural Logic of
Transnationality.* Durham, NC: Duke University Press.

Open Democracy UK (28 February 2017) "The
Strange Link Between the DUP Brexit Donation
and a Notorious Indian Gun Running Trial". By
Peter Geoghegan and Adam Ramsay. https://www.
opendemocracy.net/uk/peter-geoghegan-adam-ramsay/
mysterious-dup-brexit-donation-plot-thickens

Papastergiadis, N. (2000) *The Turbulence of Migration:
Globalization, Deterritorialization and Hybridity.*
Cambridge: Polity Press.

Progressive Unionist Party (PUP) (1 November 2002)
Principles of Loyalism: An Internal Discussion Paper. http://
www.pup-ni.org.uk/loyalism/principlesdocument.aspx

Ruddock, A. (8 January 2006) "Addicted to State
Subvention, North Will Suffer When It's Gone". *The
Times.*

Shirlow, P. (2012) *The End of Ulster Loyalism.* Manchester:
Manchester University Press.

Shirlow, P., and Murtagh, B. (2006) *Belfast: Segregation,
Violence and the City.* London: Pluto Press.

Shirlow, P., Graham, B., McEvoy, K., Ó hAdhmaill, F., and Purvis, D. (2005) *Politically Motivated Former Prisoner Groups: Community Activism and Conflict Transformation*. Belfast: Northern Ireland Community Relations Council.

Slugger O'Toole (13 October 2015) "DUP and Sinn Fein Vote Down Jim Allister's SPAD Bill". By David McCann. https://sluggerotoole.com/2015/10/13/dup-and-sinn-fein-vote-down-jim-allisters-spad-bill/

Special European Union Programmes Body (SEUPB) (2015) *Annual Report and Accounts for the Year ended 31 December 2014.*

Standing, G. (2009) *Work after Globalisation: Building Occupational Citizenship*. Northampton, MA: Edward Elgar.

Stewart, P. and McKearney, T. (2018) "The Good Friday Agreement and Britain's 'Deep State': Britain's Long Goodbye and Speedy Return". In: Grady, J., and Grocott, C. (eds.), *The Continuing Imperialism of Free Trade: Developments, Trends and the Role of Supranational Agents*. London: Routledge.

The Detail (12 September 2012) "The DUP's Full Role in Red Sky Row Revealed". By Barry McCaffrey. http://www.thedetail.tv/articles/the-dup-s-full-role-in-red-sky-row-revealed

The Detail (29 September 2016) "Stormont's Petition of Concern Used 115 Times in Five Years". By Claire Smyth. http://www.thedetail.tv/articles/stormont-s-petition-of-concern-used-115-times-in-five-years

The TUC Commission on Vulnerable Employment (2008) *Hidden Work, Hidden Lives: The Short Report of the Commission on Vulnerable Employment.* www.vulnerableworkers.org. uk/files/CoVE_short_report.pdf

The TUC Commission on Vulnerable Employment (2015) *The Decent jobs Deficit: The Human Cost of Zero-Hours Working in the UK.* https://www.tuc.org.uk/sites/default/files/DecentJobsDeficitReport_0.pdf

Tinson, A., and MacInnes, T. (15 Mar 2016) *Monitoring poverty and social exclusion in Northern Ireland 2016.* Joseph Rowntree Foundation.

Van Wanrooy, B., Bewley, H., Bryson, A., Forth, J., Freeth, S., Stokes, L., Wood, S. (2013) *The 2011 Workplace Employment Relations Study: First Findings.* https://www.workplaceleadership.com.au/publications/2011-workplace

Wallace, A., McAreavey, R., and Atkin, K. (2013) *Poverty and Ethnicity in Northern Ireland: An Evidence Review.* Belfast: Joseph Rowntree Foundation. https://www.york.ac.uk/media/chp/documents/2013/poverty-ethnicity-northern-ireland-full.pdf

Wills, J., May J., Datta, K., Evans, Y., Herbert, J., and McIlwaine, C. (2010) *Global Cities at Work: New Migrant Divisions of Labour.* London: Pluto Press.

Women's Aid Federation NI (2010) *Response to the NIO Consultation: A Bill of Rights for Northern Ireland 'Next Steps'.* Belfast: Women's Aid Federation.

Acknowledgements

Thanks are due to Laura Duffy from Armagh City for her assistance and advice on art and design. In addition, we thank Allan Cameron of Vagabond Voices for his solid commitment to this book which is based on a project exploring the changing nature of state and society in Northern Ireland since the GFA. We would also like to pay special thanks to Dana Keller for her outstanding work on the text and determination to work through a range of technical and other presentational issues as they arose. She is surely one of the best editors around today. A sincere thanks to you Dana! The authors.

About the Authors

Paul Stewart was born and brought up in Derry and Belfast, and was until recently Professor of Sociology of Work and Employment at the University of Strathclyde, where he coordinated the Marie Curie "ChangingEmployment" programme (2012–2016). He has published on the impact of sectarianism on Polish and Lithuanian migrant workers in the north of Ireland. He is a member of UNITE and a non-executive director of CAIRDE Teo, an Irish language community association in Armagh City, and a participant in the Peadar O'Donnell Socialist Republican Forum. He is co-author of *We Sell Our Time No More* (Pluto Press, 2009), and was editor of the British Sociological Association's journal *Work, Employment and Society*. He is on the editorial committee of *Capital and Class*.

Tommy McKearney is a former member of the IRA, a political ex-prisoner and hunger striker. Remaining interested in contemporary politics, he regularly contributes to media debates on Irish republican politics. He is the author of *The Provisional IRA: From Insurrection to Parliament* (Pluto Press, 2011) and writes a regular column for the monthly *Socialist Voice*. An active trade unionist, he is on the National Executive of the Independent Workers Union. He is involved in the Peadar O'Donnell Socialist Republican Forum which is building a united socialist movement in Ireland. Originally from County Tyrone, he now lives in County Monaghan in the Irish Republic.

Gearóid Ó Machail is an Executive Director of Aonach Mhacha, a collaborative cultural enterprise initiative in Armagh City. He has worked in the community sector for over twenty-five years and has established a number of worker-owned enterprises. He holds an honours degree in Social Sciences from Queens University Belfast and recently acquired an Advanced Diploma in Social Enterprise from the University of Ulster. Gearóid is an Irish language activist and is deeply involved in the Irish-medium education sector in Armagh. He is an active committee member of the Peadar O'Donnell Socialist Republican Forum and of Friends of the International Brigades in Ireland.

Patricia Campbell is from County Tyrone, a nurse by profession and President of the Independent Workers Union. She has presented at international conferences, including the American Psychological Association (APA) and a World Health Organisation (WHO) sponsored conference in Palestine in 2008. A long-term human rights campaigner and trade unionist activist, she was recognised for her lifetime human rights work when awarded the Passion for Peace Award in Philadelphia in 2015. In 2016 she co-authored *Marxism and Psychology* (ReMarx Publishing) with Susan Rosenthal. In 2017 she presented a groundbreaking paper on the psychology of torture at the renowned Adler Graduate School in Toronto.

Brian Garvey is from Armagh in the north of Ireland and now works as a Lecturer at the University of Strathclyde, Scotland, in the Department of Work and Organisation. He was previously an organiser for the Independent Workers Union in Ireland and has been involved with a range of community and labour organisations in Ireland, Scotland and Brazil. He currently represents his branch of the University and College Union.

Index